Perspectives o

ALSO BY ANDREW J. RAUSCH
AND FROM MCFARLAND

*Perspectives on Stephen King: Conversations
with Authors, Experts and Collaborators* (2019)

*Fifty Filmmakers: Conversations with Directors
from Roger Avary to Steven Zaillian* (2008)

Perspectives on Elmore Leonard

Conversations with Authors, Experts and Collaborators

ANDREW J. RAUSCH

McFarland & Company, Inc., Publishers
Jefferson, North Carolina

Library of Congress Cataloguing-in-Publication Data

Names: Rausch, Andrew J., author.
Title: Perspectives on Elmore Leonard : conversations with authors,
experts and collaborators / Andrew J. Rausch.
Description: Jefferson, North Carolina : McFarland & Company, Inc., Publishers,
2022 | Includes bibliographical references and index.
Identifiers: LCCN 2022014615 | ISBN 9781476680026 (paperback : acid free paper) ∞
ISBN 9781476646121 (ebook)
Subjects: LCSH: Leonard, Elmore, 1925-2013—Criticism and interpretation.
| BISAC: LITERARY CRITICISM / American / General
| LCGFT: Literary criticism. | Interviews
Classification: LCC PS3562.E55 Z84 2022 | DDC 813/.54—dc23/eng/20220411
LC record available at https://lccn.loc.gov/2022014615

British Library cataloguing data are available

ISBN (print) 978-1-4766-8002-6
ISBN (ebook) 978-1-4766-4612-1

© 2022 Andrew J. Rausch. All rights reserved

*No part of this book may be reproduced or transmitted in any form
or by any means, electronic or mechanical, including photocopying
or recording, or by any information storage and retrieval system,
without permission in writing from the publisher.*

Front cover image: Elmore Leonard, 1985 (Photofest)

Printed in the United States of America

*McFarland & Company, Inc., Publishers
Box 611, Jefferson, North Carolina 28640
www.mcfarlandpub.com*

Table of Contents

Table of Contents

Introduction

Elmore Leonard—As American as Jazz

One trait all literary giants share is that they have a distinct voice and writing style. That might seem like a given, but the majority of published authors don't have the kind of unique voice that would allow a person to read five pages of any given novel and then be able to instantly identify him or her. But Elmore Leonard has a voice that is distinct, original, and immediately recognizable. Although Leonard has spawned his share of imitators, his prose still stands out distinctively when read alongside them.

Time magazine once dubbed Leonard the "Dickens of Detroit," a snazzy title that ultimately stuck. Leonard himself was skeptical of the title and once questioned what his nickname might have been had he lived in Buffalo. To this, the British novelist, essayist, and Leonard admirer Martin Amis joked that he might have been the "Balzac of Buffalo." Jokes aside, it is Amis himself who has provided the best defense of the title, asserting that Leonard was "as close as anything you have here in America to a national novelist, a concept that almost seemed to die with Charles Dickens but has here been revived."

In the spirit (and stereotype) of being labeled the essential American writer, Leonard's works have been linked to Hollywood almost from the start. Leonard always exhibited a knack for crafting scenes in a cinematic manner; when the reader experiences them, he or she "sees" the scenes inside their head as if they were watching a movie. This is one reason Leonard's stories and novels have long been favorites for film adaptation. At their best (e.g. Scott Frank), film adapters are able to simply take what Leonard has written and transfer it almost directly to screenplay form with very little additional material needed. Of course, Hollywood has a long-standing predilection for tinkering with source material, and adapters frequently feel they must transform the existing property into something new and different. This can work if the

1

Introduction

screenwriter is a writer of Leonard's caliber (e.g. Quentin Tarantino), but very few are. This is one of the reasons most of the adaptations don't work—they fail to capture the essence and feel of Elmore Leonard.

The cinematic nature of Leonard's writing was apparent from the start, as one of his earliest published stories, "3:10 to Yuma" (*Dime Western Magazine*, March 1953), was secured by Columbia Pictures for adaptation. This was followed by the sale of a second story, "The Captives" (*Argosy*, February 1955), which was adapted as *The Tall T* (1957), part of Budd Boetticher and Randolph Scott's legendary "Ranown Cycle." (Although they created in different mediums, Boetticher was similar to Leonard in that he managed to craft true art in what was considered a lowbrow form; for Boetticher it was directing the "B" motion picture, for Leonard it was writing "genre" fiction.)

Leonard was still working full-time in advertising during his first decade as a published writer. Imagine Leonard, still working his mundane day-to-day job and having not one but *two* exceptional films adapted from his work and released in 1957. (Those films, *3:10 to Yuma* and *The Tall T*, are still considered two of the finest Leonard adaptations.) One would think this would be somewhat of a shock to Leonard, who saw himself as a blue-collar everyman, but one gets the distinct feeling he was largely unimpressed with these successes. (They certainly didn't change him.) Even if he wasn't yet recognized as an elite literary figure by 1957, the writing was clearly on the wall that he was an extraordinary talent.

Leonard's stories were quite different in the 1950s from those most people associate with his name today. In the early days of his career, Leonard wrote Westerns rather than crime/noir. Westerns were prevalent on television and in magazines and novels at the time, so his decision to write in the genre came more from practicality than passion. That he could simply select a genre for practical reasons and then excel within it is telling of his talent. Leonard wrote five Western novels between 1953 and 1961 (*The Bounty Hunters*, 1953, *The Law at Randado*, 1954, *Escape from Five Shadows*, 1956, *Last Stand at Saber River*, 1959, and *Hombre*, 1961). After Leonard published *Hombre*, his agent, H.N. Swanson, informed him that the Western genre was drying up and advised him to find a new genre. As we all know, Leonard then moved into the crime genre, which was somewhat of a lateral move and perhaps a logical transition considering the similarities of the genres.

I mentioned the cinematic nature of Leonard's work a few paragraphs back. So, what is it that makes Leonard's work more cinematic than that of other talented contemporaries? For starters, his books are divided into scenes, similar to the way films are structured. He also has a (deceptively) simplistic way of describing things that still manages to paint a vivid picture in the reader's mind. Instead of spending three paragraphs describing a character's physical appearance, their clothing, and the settings in detail the way most writers do, Leonard gets right to the point. Similar to Ernest Hemingway, Leonard pared his prose down to the bone, utilizing an unmatched economy of language and excising anything he didn't deem absolutely necessary. Or, as he wrote in his famous "10 Rules for Writing" (*Detroit Free Press*, 2010), he "[tried] to leave out the parts that readers tend to skip." Leonard was keenly aware that readers rarely skip or skim over dialogue, so he constructed his stories around it.

Leonard's dialogue is the primary reason Hollywood loves his work. He had an uncanny ear for dialogue. He didn't just fill the pages of his novels with dialogue, he filled them with *extraordinary* dialogue that crackled and leaped from the page. While the dialogue in Leonard's '50s and '60s work was adequate, it was more utilitarian than the dialogue he would craft in his post–1970 crime novels. Inspired by the language and cadence of the hoods in George V. Higgins' *The Friends of Eddie Coyle* (1970), Leonard's own characters' rhythms and speech patterns changed dramatically.

However, it must be noted that, despite his being heavily influenced by *Coyle*, Leonard's dialogue was something completely different from Higgins'. While *Coyle*'s characters use verbiage that has the air of authenticity and speak in a cadence that is undeniably unique and distinguishable, Leonard's (mid–1970s and beyond) characters speak in a more heightened, flavorful way. They also engage in back-and-forth conversation instead of delivering the kind of long-winded monologues Higgins is known for. Leonard's characters speak in a way that *feels* authentic but is hyper-stylized. There have been many talented wordsmiths writing in a variety of mediums who have crafted their own distinct brand of colorful, stylized banter (Tarantino, Charlie Stella, David Mamet, Shane Black, Joe R. Lansdale, etc.), but Leonard is arguably the finest. (Perhaps Leonard ties Higgins at the peak of his powers, but Higgins seemed to lose his gift for gab after his first couple of crime outings. After that, his work reads as if he was trying to recapture the voice he'd once possessed.) When Leonard's characters speak, the dialogue never sounds forced and he rarely (if ever) hits a false note. In addition to the melodic cadence of his dialogue, he had a unique talent for conveying the necessary description of character and place within it.

With his work frequently adapted to screen (both small and large) and his name consistently appearing on the *New York Times* bestsellers list, it could be tempting for the casual observer to lump Leonard in with popular authors like John Grisham, Danielle Steel, or James Patterson, but that would be grossly inaccurate and unfathomably unjust. There is something special about Elmore Leonard. He, like Stephen King, walked with one foot in the pop world and the other in the literary, and did so without falling. And although they swim in the same waters of mass popularity as countless lessers, King and Leonard are separated from them by an important distinction: they possess(ed) undeniable talent and, although they are prolific enough to raise the eyebrows of naysayers and also work in genres considered lowbrow, their efforts have significantly impacted and elevated the genres in which they wrote. (Both have written in multiple genres, but I'm speaking here to those they are synonymous with.)

Leonard, like any writer, was not without weaknesses. For starters, his plots are secondary to the dialogue itself (the plots were a "mechanism to get his characters talking," observed *The Guardian's* Mark Lawson). Then there's the fact that a great many of his protagonists are interchangeable or extremely close to being so. The aforementioned Martin Amis once wrote, "[Leonard] occasionally used the same character in more than one novel, and admitted to me that his main character was often 'the same guy with a different name.' That guy was a tarnished hero, usually but not invariably male, unafraid to break the law but with a fundamental sense of decency, if not of legality." Why would Leonard essentially write the same character with different names in different novels? One reason could be the familiarity and ease in writing about characters he already knew well, but it is likely there is a different reason. The great crime writer Lawrence Block once told me a story about Leonard's agent (the aforementioned Swanson) advising him not to write a series about a singular character because doing such would lose potential film option revenue (a likely single option for a series character as opposed to multiple options for different standalones). According to Block, Leonard once told Swanson he wanted to write another book about his *The Big Bounce* (1969) protagonist, Jack Ryan. To this, Block says the agent told Leonard, "Write anything you want, kid, but make sure you call him something else."

Much has been written here and elsewhere regarding his gift for crafting dialogue, but Leonard was no one-trick pony possessing a single talent. Leonard was a stylist with a variety of literary flourishes in his arsenal. Perhaps the most significant of these is his "invention of a present tense indefinitely suspended" (Amis, *Inside Story*, 2020), which has also been called "the Elmore Leonard tense." Amis first highlighted this in his review for *Riding the Rap* (1995): "[T]he essence of Elmore is to be found in his use of the present participle. What this means, in effect, is that he had discovered a way of slowing down and suspending the English sentence—or let's say the American sentence, because Mr. Leonard is as American as jazz. Instead of writing 'Warren Ganz III lived up in Manalpan, Palm Beach County,' Mr. Leonard writes: 'Warren Ganz III, living up in Manalpan, Palm Beach County.' He writes, 'Bobby saying,' and then opens quotes. He writes, 'Dawn saying,' and then opens quotes. We are not in the imperfect tense (Dawn was saying) or the present tense (Dawn says) or the historic present (Dawn said). We are in a kind of marijuana tense (Dawn saying), creamy, wandering, weak-verbed. Such sentences seem to open up a lag in time, through which Mr. Leonard easily slides, gaining entry to his players' hidden minds. He doesn't just show you what these people say and do. He shows you where they breathe."

The truth is, at the end of the day, the primary aspect of Leonard's writing that made him as popular as he was/is, is also an element that perhaps causes some champions of highbrow "literary" writing (i.e., "the academy") to dismiss him. That is Leonard's primary goal (and one at which he succeeded) being that he remain "invisible"; where most so-called literary writers purposely write in a manner that draws attention to the craftsmanship behind it (verbiage, sentence structure, metaphors, etc.), he sought to write in a way in which his contributions were obscured and hopefully forgotten by the reader. He never wanted the reader to encounter a line or word that reminded them that there was a god at a typewriter creating it all.

There is far less debate regarding Leonard's "street cred" as a "serious" writer today. (There was never a shred of doubt for me, which is why I'm reluctant to stop arguing his importance.) In fact, in the preface to his excellent study, *Being Cool: The Work of Elmore Leonard* (The Johns Hopkins University Press, 2013), Leonard expert Charles J. Rzepka declares, "The debate is over. Admirers now include Martin Amis, Walker Percy, Ann Beattie, and former poet laureate Robert Pinsky. Saul Bellow was a fan and Leonard has even been mentioned in the same breath as 'experimental writers' like Pirandello, Calvino,

Introduction

Robbe-Grillet, Borges, and Nabokov. Both the topical reach of his work and the span of his career and canon are enormous: six decades, dozens of short stories, and forty-five novels, not to mention movies, screenplays, and televised versions of his writings."

Giving credence to Rzepka's assertion is the fact that *Perspectives on Elmore Leonard: Conversations with Authors, Experts and Collaborators* is the sixth full-length (American) volume devoted solely to Leonard and his writings. It is not intended to be the definitive study on the subject. Excellent tomes by James E. Devlin, David Geherin, Rzepka, and Paul Challen precede it. With the addition of each new study, additional information comes to light, giving us a more complete picture of the author. As such, the present work should be viewed as a supplemental volume intended to spark dialogue while providing details that will hopefully provide additional clarity.

Published Works of Elmore Leonard

Novels

The Bounty Hunters (1953)
The Law at Randado (1954)
Escape from Five Shadows (1956)
Last Stand at Saber River (1959)
Hombre (1961)
The Big Bounce (1969)
The Moonshine War (1969)
Valdez Is Coming (1970)
Forty Lashes Less One (1972)
Mr. Majestyk (1974)
Fifty-Two Pickup (1974)
Swag (1976)
Unknown Man No. 89 (1977)
The Hunted (1977)
The Switch (1978)
Gunsights (1979)
City Primeval (1980)
Gold Coast (1980)
Split Images (1981)
Cat Chaser (1982)
Stick (1983)
LaBrava (1983)

Glitz (1985)
Bandits (1987)
Touch (1987)
Freaky Deaky (1988)
Killshot (1989)
Get Shorty (1990)
Maximum Bob (1991)
Rum Punch (1992)
Pronto (1993)
Riding the Rap (1995)
Out of Sight (1996)
Cuba Libre (1998)
Be Cool (1999)
Pagan Babies (2000)
Tishomingo Blues (2002)
Mr. Paradise (2004)
The Hot Kid (2005)
Comfort to the Enemy (2006)
Up in Honey's Room (2007)
Road Dogs (2009)
Djibouti (2010)
Raylan (2012)

Short Story Collections

The Tonto Woman and Other Western Stories (1998)
When the Women Come Out to Dance (2002)
The Complete Western Stories of Elmore Leonard (2004)
Moment of Vengeance and Other Stories (2006)
Blood Money and Other Stories (2006)
Three-Ten to Yuma and Other Stories (2006)
Trail of the Apache and Other Stories (2007)
Comfort to the Enemy and Other Carl Webster Stories (2009)
Fire in the Hole (2012)
Charlie Martz and Other Stories: The Unpublished Stories of Elmore Leonard (2014)

Published Works of Elmore Leonard

Nonfiction

Notebooks (1991)
10 Rules of Writing (2007)

Children's Books

A Coyote's In the House (2004)

Screenplays

The Moonshine War (1970)
Joe Kidd (1972)
Mr. Majestyk (1974)
High Noon, Part II: The Return of Will Kane (1980)
Stick (1985)
52 Pick-Up (1986)
Desperado (1987)
The Rosary Murders (1987)
The Return of Desperado (1988)
Cat Chaser (1989)

1

Charles Ardai

Born in New York City the son of Holocaust survivors, Charles Ardai grew up hearing the grim stories of his parents' struggles. These hardscrabble tales would perhaps play some role in Ardai's eventual fascination with the hardboiled crime stories published in the lurid paperbacks of yesteryear. He would later apply these pulp elements to his own fiction, which would appear in such publications as *Ellery Queen's Mystery Magazine* and *Alfred Hitchcock's Mystery Magazine*, as well as a number of anthologies. Ardai also made a name for himself in 1996 as one of the founders of the internet provider Juno.

In 2004, Ardai, along with his partner-in-crime Max Phillips, established Hard Case Crime, a publishing imprint created to recreate the sorts of crime novels he himself enjoyed, complete with suggestive painted covers. Under the Hard Case Crime banner, Ardai published his own debut novel, *Little Girl Lost* (2004), which he wrote under the pseudonym Richard Aleas. The breakthrough novel would be nominated for both the Edgar Allan Poe Award and the Shamus Award. With Hard Case Crime, Ardai and Phillips would ultimately publish both new crime fiction (including three Stephen King novels) and reprints of more obscure novels by the likes of Lawrence Block, Donald Westlake, and Harlan Ellison.

Hard Case Crime has published nearly 100 novels (to date) and Ardai himself has penned the novels *Songs of Innocence* (2007), *Fifty-to-One* (2008), and *Hunt Through the Cradle of Fear* (2009), as well as the novelization of the Shane Black motion picture *The Nice Guys* (2016).

Although he hasn't published any of Elmore Leonard's novels, author/publisher/editor Ardai certainly has the credentials to be considered an expert on the genre.

ANDREW J. RAUSCH: *Are you a fan of Elmore Leonard's work?*

CHARLES ARDAI: There was a time when I read a lot of Elmore

Leonard novels back to back. He was still alive and publishing, so when he published a new book I'd get it in hardcover. Meanwhile, I went back through his backlist and had an enormous amount of fun.

Then I started Hard Case Crime with Max Phillips, my partner in this crazy adventure that's now gone on for fifteen years. Max introduced me to Elmore Leonard and handed me used paperback copies of books like *Stick* (1983) and *Glitz (1985)* and *Gold Coast* (1980) after he finished reading them. He wouldn't have passed them to me if he didn't love them, and then I read them and loved them.

The thing is, here we are 15 or 20 years later, and I can't remember a single thing about any of the books. I remember loving them. I remember reading and enjoying them. I don't remember the characters' names. I don't remember the plot. I remember the general atmosphere, the general tone. I remember the dialogue being awfully witty, and I remember some of the plot developments being very satisfying, but if you put a gun to my head, I couldn't tell you what happened.

That's a very interesting thing. It's different from not remembering the exact details of the plot in *The Big Sleep* (1939), which Raymond Chandler himself couldn't have told you himself the day he finished writing it. I remember Philip Marlowe, the character, I remember the general story with his wheelchair, and I remember the daughter who throws herself into Philip Marlowe's arms. So even if I don't remember who got killed and exactly why and where, I remember a lot of the plot of *The Big Sleep.* I could not tell you that about any of Leonard's books. Ever since you contacted me, I've been considering that. Why is that? Here he is, an incredibly gifted writer. On a sentence-to-sentence basis, what some would call his micro writing, is exceptional. But the macro writing, the stuff that operates at the level of an entire story or an entire book.... Why is that so evanescent for me? Why does that vanish from my head like dew from a blade of grass? It may say more about me than him, but it's interesting to me. He feels, to me, like a genuine pleasure from an earlier time that served its purpose, and is no more. A little bit like remembering summer ice cream in the winter.

Nobody I've spoken to (thus far) seems to be able to point at a specific Leonard novel as being his masterpiece. Do you have any thoughts on that?

CA: Well, he never developed a single character who became his dominant mouthpiece in his fiction, the way [Raymond] Chandler had Philip Marlowe or any number of other writers had a single dominant character; the ultimate example being [Arthur] Conan Doyle with Sherlock Holmes. So, I think picking a single character or a single novel is hard, even though Leonard did have interesting characters. Chili Palmer came in two books [*Get Shorty*, 1990, and *Be Cool*, 1999]. Raylan Givens came back in a few ["Fire in the Hole," 2001, *Pronto*, 1993, *Riding the Rap*, 1995, and *Raylan*, 2012]. He used a single character for multiple books, but no one that completely dominated. That's a blessing for writers sometimes. I think sometimes writers think it's a curse to be associated too strongly with one character and not free to spread his wings and do other things. It's freeing for a writer during his life, but after his death it's limiting in terms of posterity.

In terms of one book, I think his most famous is clearly *Get Shorty*, and it's mostly because of the movie. I think *Rum Punch* (1992), of course, became the Tarantino movie [*Jackie Brown*, 1997], but I still think if you had to pick one book that was the famous one, it would be *Get Shorty*. The funny thing is, *Get Shorty* is not my favorite, by any means. I read it after it had already become famous, so I had high expectations. But I remember when I got to the end I thought, "eh, it's fine." It was entertaining while it went, but I didn't think it was anything special. The basic premise that the film business and organized crime had something in common just felt ... not false, but a little facile. It's not like that insight was so shattering that I did backflips in the face of it.

On the other hand, I do remember some of his early, very tight—I suspect they were paperback originals, but I don't know that for a fact—books like *Gold Coast* (1980) and *Stick*. Even though I don't remember the plots well, I remember thinking they were truly exceptional novels. I don't remember feeling that way about any of the ones that came out late in his life. I would buy them in bookstores and read them, sort of dutifully more than with overwhelming enthusiasm. I would enjoy them but not love them. By the time you got to *Rum Punch* and some of the later ones, they were fun, but they didn't feel magnificent.

I think his older novels had a kind of purity to them that was beautiful. It was just so sharp and to the bone. There was not an ounce of fat on them. Even among those, I find it hard to pick just one and say that was the masterpiece and the others were less. I think that was the period when his writing was at his strongest. If I was going to give a friend some Leonards to read, that's where I would start. I would go back to the 1970s books. He did start earlier, but he started with Westerns. I've never read any of his Westerns beyond some of his crime novels that have a guy with a cowboy hat in them.

Perspectives on Elmore Leonard

I will say that there were some books I considered particularly weak. I'll tell you the history of one. At one point, when we started Hard Case Crime, I liked the idea of getting one of Leonard's books into our line. He was an important author and one that I did love at the time. I reached out to him, and he sent a very nice letter back. It was very brief, but it was a nice one. I had described to him what we were doing—trying to revive the style of the old paperback—and he was talking about how.... I'm trying to remember exactly what he said, but as I recall, he said he used to read John D. MacDonald. He didn't remember a lot of authors, but ironically, he said something not very different from what I'm saying about him; that he didn't remember a lot of authors from that period, even though he read plenty. I'm trying to remember if he said he liked John D. MacDonald but not Erle Stanley Gardner, or if it was the other way around. He was generally supportive of the idea of Hard Case Crime, but didn't go out of his way to participate, which is totally fine.

I then went to his catalog of books to try and find any books of his that were out of print. Already by then, I think Harper was his publisher and had not brought out the uniform set of big paperbacks that were very much a series. I could only find two, if I remember correctly, that were not in print. I immediately bought and read those two, thinking maybe one of those was good. And they weren't. One of those was called *The Moonshine War* (1969). That was his attempt at some sort of hillbilly, backwoods, stills and rifles romp. The other one was *Unknown Man No. 89* (1977). I read it and I thought, that one's not very good either. Those two, unfortunately, the only two I might have a chance to buy the rights to, weren't good. So I gave up on acquiring a Leonard novel. Then eventually, Harper brought them back into print. It was moot. I wouldn't have succeeded, even if I had tried.

On the other hand, another one in that category, when I was buying the new books as they came into print, was one called *Cuba Libre* (1998), which was an historical novel; it wasn't set in the present. I found it absolutely unreadable. I don't know how other people feel about that one. I've never gone and looked it up. But I remember getting stuck after one or two chapters. And Leonard's books, whatever they were, they were never unreadable. They were always highly readable. And for some reason, that one, I just couldn't get into. It made me think that maybe, even though it hearkened back to his Western writing style, maybe writing period novels was not his thing. Maybe he needed it to be modern. Or maybe it's just because I don't like Westerns.

Those were the three negatives. I can't think of another Leonard novel that I didn't enjoy, to one extent or another. I'm an enthusiast. If pressed, I would say I'm a proselytizer. I have certainly turned other people on to him. But that's where I get stuck. I find myself saying all those good things and then not following through with the real conviction that would come with being able to say, "Here's the book you should read and why."

I guess in a pinch, I would point to either *Gold Coast* or *Stick* because I remember when Max Phillips handed them to me, and I remember really loving both of them.

You mentioned not enjoying his later novels as much. Do you think some of the edge was gone in those? It seems like a lot of authors eventually lose at least some of their edge. Like Stephen King, whom you've edited. I feel like his writing has become more polished and precise, but some of the edge from his early work is gone.

CA: It's definitely true that writers lose edge over time. No question about that. I think as you get older, if you're a successful writer, some of the hunger goes. You're literally hungry in the early days. There's no time to write. There's a bill collector knocking at your door, and you've got a nine-to-five and you've got to cram your writing in before you fall asleep. I think some of the literal edge goes, and some of it is probably just the waning of powers as one gets older. But in the case of Leonard, it's interesting. I think he had an enormous amount of polish even in his earlier years. I don't think he got more polished. I think what Leonard became in his later years was more garrulous. So as his length increased—even in the late years, the books were often published with very large type size. Because the publisher wanted to conceal the fact that the books were actually quite short. He wasn't writing 100,000 word books generally. He was still working in the mode he started in, which was probably like a 75,000 word book. So they used large type to get the book up to 350 pages, even though it was really a 200 page book.

But it felt like he had become famous for a certain kind of character, the quirky criminal. And a certain kind of dialogue spoken by that character. So his dialogue scenes would sometimes get longer and quirkier. Of course, Tarantino was inspired by him, rather than the other way around, so calling it Tarantinoesque is completely inappropriate, but you sometimes would have dialogue scenes where the chief pleasure the author seems to be taking is in the baroque dialogue for its own sake, rather than its function in advancing the story or revealing the characters. So I remember sometimes enjoying, again, line by line, the gags,

13

the jokes, the enjoyable repartee, but feeling it was going on a bit long. I think that became more of an issue in the later years.

There was, I believe, at least one earlier novel where he did some of that, but my sense of it is that it was more self-delight in the later years and more purposeful and functional in the earlier years. Maybe it's true that there was sort of a lean and mean quality in the earlier books that made you feel you really were inhabiting a dirty world; a funny one that's served with sardonic humor, but it was a dirty, deadly place where lots of bad things happened. And it had a kind of mean quality to it. In the later books, I somehow felt it was all a little bit more affectionate. People still got shot and killed, but it felt like the balance had slightly shifted toward the comical and away from the crime element. That's a gut-level sense.

I can speak about Elmore Leonard perhaps most usefully wearing my editor's hat. It's as an editor that I can talk about his influence, and the reason I can is I get a thousand submissions of manuscripts a year. A thousand is probably a low estimate, but somewhere in the neighborhood of a thousand. Easily, 40 percent of them are trying to do Elmore Leonard. That is a lasting influence! That means that a whole generation of writers, readers, would-be writers grew up reading your work and loved it so much that they patterned their own art after yours. They, by and large, don't do it as well as you did it—even you didn't do it at the end of your life as well as you did at the start—but they all wish they could read one more great Elmore Leonard book. And because they can't get one from you, they sit down and try to write one themselves. And that really does say something about the extent of your influence. And I think Elmore Leonard did have an enormous influence in a way that only a handful of other writers have.

There's a sort of narrow coterie of passionate fans of James Ellroy who try to do an Ellroy-style word jazz thing. I'll get one submission like that every two weeks. But I'll get an Elmore Leonard knock-off every day. Rarely a day goes by that I don't get at least one book that was inspired deeply by Elmore Leonard. Maybe also by other people. The cliché of the noir hardboiled book is still based mostly on the Hammett and Chandler image of a gumshoe with the whiskey bottle in his bottom desk drawer, the trench coat and fedora hat, the beautiful dame that knocks at the door. And you do still see that sometimes. But the Elmore Leonard world of dirty cops and whimsical crooks and amusing characters of other descriptions.... I would say Leonard is the successor in many ways to Damon Runyon, whose stories inspired the musical *Guys and Dolls* (1950).

1. Charles Ardai

In the twenties, Runyon cataloged the adventures of amusingly nicknamed gangsters and cops and molls and made the world of crime a source of amusement for readers. I think, until Elmore Leonard came along, nobody else had done it quite that way. Leonard was basically doing a Damon Runyon type thing only in Florida instead of on Broadway, and with cocaine and automatic weapons instead of spats and Marlon Brando for the singing. Even Elmore Leonard didn't come out of nowhere, but people really responded to him, so you have another generation of published writers who are doing things that maybe they never would've thought to do if it wasn't for Leonard. Guys like Charlie Stella. They're very funny, they're charming, they're funny crook novels. I don't know that they would've written those books if it weren't for Leonard.

It's like the dark matter in the universe—what's all the mass you can't see? The number of books that are in bookstores and on library shelves that resemble Leonard pale in significance in comparison to the vast number that have never gotten published, that only an editor who sees the slush pile sees. I can tell you that however influential Leonard was with other professional writers, he was vastly influential with the unpublished masses who continue to write Elmore Leonard pastiches every day. Sometimes when they submit the books they even acknowledge him. "This is like a cross between Elmore Leonard and...." Sadly, they just, by and large, don't do it as well as the master did. But that's okay. But the echoes of his writing are still being heard in the dark alleyways of the crime genre.

I do notice some similarities to Leonard in the Jason Starr/Ken Bruen "Bust" series you've published. I think it's because of Jason Starr's contributions, as he has stated publicly that Leonard influenced his writing.

CA: I think you're right. Those four books, *Bust* (2006), *Slide* (2007), *The Max* (2008), and *Pimp* (2016), are the only ones I can remember where Jason has allowed himself to be light. If you read his other books, they're deadly serious and they're a lot more in the vein of David Goodis or Jim Thompson, where there's somebody who's leading a difficult, problematic life and it gets worse and worse and spirals into utter disaster, often thanks to his own misdeeds. In the books he wrote with Ken, he allowed himself to have fun. They're full of violence, full of bad things happening, but observed through a comic lens. Yes, I think there's some of Elmore Leonard there. I think he had a lot of fun writing them in part because it was fun for him to be a little different from what he normally does.

I'll point to another one that you might take a look at, that's not as widely known. We published it our first year. I think it was possibly our 12th book, called *Dutch Uncle* (2011). It's kind of relevant here. It's by Peter Pavia, who is a passionate fan of Elmore Leonard. He wrote a story about crooks of various distorts, intersecting their lives, careening around each other in Florida. And it's not an accident that the title of the book, *Dutch Uncle*, includes a reference to Dutch Leonard's nickname.

The provenance of that book was, I was trying to get the rights to reprint a book by Erle Stanley Gardner. I didn't know who handled the Gardner estate. I found that it was handled by a man named Larry Hughes. Now, Larry Hughes, I think, was Erle Stanley Gardner's publisher once upon a time, maybe 80 years prior. He was very old by the time I spoke to him. I think handling the Gardner estate was one of the last things he did. While I had him on the phone talking about publishing a Gardner book, he said, "Somebody sent me his manuscript, telling me it was really good and I should read it. It was really good, but I don't know what to do with it. Would you take a look?" That was *Dutch Uncle*. I read it and thought, this is great. This is about as good as Elmore Leonard! It was one of the rare cases where someone did an Elmore Leonard pastiche that was actually as good as Elmore Leonard. I was very excited, so I went ahead and published it. It didn't make a huge splash. I think maybe 10,000 people read it, and now maybe four or five copies a year get sold. It's not very much. But you might enjoy it as an example of a latter-day Elmore Leonard–inspired book.

But that was a stab at doing something more or less explicitly Leonard inspired. And people did like it. It got good reviews and it was generally, by our standards, a success. I think since then we haven't done anything that is precisely a Leonard-y thing. One of the reasons I explain to people when they make submissions is, anything I see a lot of, I don't want to buy. Because I know I'm going to see ten more like it in the next few weeks and ten more a few weeks after that. You'd really have to stand out in a big way, because why should I buy this one if I'll see ten more next week? I generally don't buy books about cleverly named serial killers being pursued by FBI profilers just because there's a million of those books with nothing that makes them stand out more than others. Now, if Thomas Harris came around and wanted to write me one, that's different!

It's similar with stories about the Russian mob and human trafficking.... We've seen too many of those. So anytime I see a book that's clearly doing Elmore Leonard, I more or less turn it down instantly because there's just too much of that.

It's a strange thing that Hard Case Crime, which would be a natural home for Elmore Leonard–type fiction, actually has very little of it because I see so much of it. I'm much more likely to buy and publish a book that is different from everything else I'm seeing than one that is like a lot of the things I'm seeing, even though the fact that something is done a lot is probably a sign that it would be popular. It's a sign that readers crave it. The thing that is different might actually be different because no one wants it! If only one author in the world wants to write it, maybe no one wants to read it! Maybe it's my own perversity, but I'm much more likely to buy something that's unlike anything else than something that is like a lot of things. I think in some ways, Elmore Leonard survives as a photocopy of a photocopy in the dimension of style. Everyone kind of has a gut-level recollection of what Elmore Leonard's style was, and they mostly don't remember it being quite as absurd and quite as sharp and cunning and quite as good as it really was. They just have some vague memory of Tarantino's crooks saying funny things to each other.

Maybe this will be my excuse to do a reread of some of Leonard's best books. I kind of miss them. I remember them being a little dangerous. I remember them being a little shocking. And yet when I think of Leonard, I think of someone fairly comfortable. Fairly tame. Sort of amusing. And he was not a cozy writer. Funny, but not a cozy writer. I think the passing of time may have mellowed his reputation, and maybe it's time to reclaim Leonard for the scrappy alley-fighter he actually was, rather than the cool, avuncular, beret-wearing jazzbo he came across as later in his life.

To what do you attribute Leonard's rising to greater prominence than some of the other great crime writers of his generation?

CA: Why did he become even bigger even than guys like Lawrence Block, Donald Westlake, Ed McBain? McBain was probably the next one down. He had a lot of success. His name was widely known by the public, but not as big as Elmore Leonard. Block and Westlake would be maybe one notch down in terms of commercial success, as well.

I think the movies have an awful lot to do with that. Not to say McBain didn't have his share of adaptations. There was the *87th Precinct* (1961) series, although it didn't last long. There was a point at which, similar to King, you just knew that when Leonard published a book, it was shortly going to become a movie.

Perspectives on Elmore Leonard

So you ask, why is that? Yes, the fact that he had a lot of movies made is why more people knew his name. But why did he have a lot of movies made? Something about his work felt more cinematic, so what is that? His books sometimes had a bit more of a thriller-y element to them rather than pure detection. It wasn't "the crime has already been committed and the detective is interviewing random people to find out why it happened"; the backwards-looking narrative of a mystery. His books often had the propulsive forward-looking quality of a movie-thriller, which is "a bunch of people are putting in motion a plan, things are going to go awry in interesting ways and we, in real time, will see these things happen and they often involve drugs, guns, beautiful women, car chases, people getting stuck in trunks of cars, people getting gagged with duct tape." All of these things that are fun and much more exciting to see on the screen than a detective interviewing a suspect.

I think the clever dialogue had something to do with it, too. That's not to say that Westlake and Block and McBain didn't have clever dialogue, because they did. But there was something sort of punchy and Hollywood-flavored about Leonard's dialogue that suited the movie screen well. So the combination of propulsive plot, good action, forward-, rather than backward-directed plot and tight dialogue probably made it pretty easy for movie adaptations to happen. And then there's the random chance of it started happening for him, so he had momentum, so it kept happening for him. Sometimes you get lucky the first time and that's all it takes. But also, who was his agent? Was his agent better connected in Hollywood than Don Westlake's agent? Anything's possible.

Whatever accounted for it, I think the movie connection was a big part of why people thought of him as a big deal; as one of the big authors at the time. Because you always saw one of his movies on the multiplex screen, even if the movie wasn't very successful, like Roy Scheider and Ann-Margret in *52 Pick-Up* (1986). That was a movie where it wasn't a big success. It came and went. But there was one like it pretty much every year, or every other year! It felt like there was always an Elmore Leonard adaptation.

Just like it felt like, until recently, that there was always a King adaptation every year. But now, with Stephen King's work, it's vastly greater than that. Now, at any given time, there are five Stephen King adaptations between TV and streaming and film. So now it's unlike anything anyone has ever seen before, where literally every book in his catalogue has been adapted and oftentimes multiple of them are available at the same time. It's gone into hyper-drive. So I think Steve is in a category all of his own.

But think of a writer like Dan Brown. Dan Brown has not generally been critically well-received, although lots of individual readers love his books. Part of what makes Dan Brown Dan Brown is the random lightning in a bottle effect of *The Da Vinci Code* (2003) becoming a bestseller. Ever since then, there have been movies, more or less, out of all his books. That's sort of self-reinforcing. Dan Brown is big in part because he's big. That's just picking one example.

Robert B. Parker. Why was he bigger than Ed McBain? Well, he had the TV series *Spenser: For Hire* (1985) with Robert Urich. And that partly made him big because Robert B. Parker was in everyone's living room once a week for years and years. Why was Erle Stanley Gardner as big as he was? Perry Mason. Why was Perry Mason big? Because he was on TV.

I think the TV and film element of Leonard's success cannot be overstated, and then it's a question of, did he deserve it more than these other writers? No. I love Larry Block's work. I think it should be on TV every day, too. But Leonard got lucky and he got some good movies made, and had representation in Hollywood. Larry had a couple of movies made and they were totally terrible. He'll be the first to tell you, and he never quite took off in the same way.

Leonard has been begrudgingly accepted in literary circles in the last few years. Why do you think they accept him in a way that's not often afforded crime writers? There are a few, like Chandler, Hammett ... but beyond that, not many.

CA: Chandler, Hammett, maybe Cain, and when we're thinking of bigger people, some people would say George V. Higgins. And that gets closer to Leonard, because what made Higgins come to the attention of the academy is his work as a stylist and his use of dialogue to propel stories. I think Leonard is much the same thing. Leonard used prose in a novel-seeming and interesting way.

Professors have become less stodgy in the last two decades and want to appear cool, hip, and with it. They want to assign more recent books and pop culture-y books to their students, and books that will entertain and not bore their students. God knows Leonard's books will entertain! They're also relatively short and quick reads, so you're not assigning somebody an 800-page doorstop.

In terms of instruction, as a professor, you want to teach people about ways of telling stories. How do you construct a story? How do you make a story move from point A to point B? Leonard is a terrific example of that and, again, part of that is what I sometimes think of as the drunk searching for his keys under the streetlight; we all know where he dropped them, but at least there's light under the streetlight, so that's where you look. Why do people assign Leonard? Because people assign Leonard. That's a name they've heard of. The books are in print and available. If you want to assign David Goodis, most of them are not in print. Most of them are not available. Maybe if you're a random professor and you're not a specialist in this particular genre, you haven't even heard of David Goodis, much less someone like Ed Lacy, who is truly forgotten.

You say, "I want a crime novelist because I want to balance out all my boring literary guys, and maybe I don't want to do the cliche thing with Chandler and Hammet. I want to do something a little different. Who else have I heard of?" Everyone's heard of Leonard. You could say why Leonard and not Robert B. Parker? I think the sense is that Leonard was a better writer. I think at his best, that's true. I think Parker was very readable, but I think Leonard was doing something a little bit more novel and interesting and accomplished. I think Elroy is another writer some academics have put on the syllabus and, again, it's for using language in certain novel ways.

I wonder if the Leonard trend will last much longer. It feels to me, at least with Ellroy, and by the way I don't like Ellroy's books nearly as much as Leonard's, but at least with Ellroy, it's not just a stylistic thing he's doing. He's got some commentary on the ills of society, on racism, on topics that might be of interest to an academic. Whereas Leonard is using his enormous talent mostly just to entertain. I couldn't point to one of his books that actually had meaning aside from being an entertaining crime novel; a higher purpose. The closest you might come is *Get Shorty* with "business is not that different from crime," but again, that's sort of an obvious message.

I think something like *L.A. Confidential* (1990) is more likely to show up on syllabuses in 20 years than *52 Pickup*, but who knows. It's kind of a fool's game to guess what will happen in 20 years. I think part of the reason is just that he's someone the professors have heard of that has a seal of approval in terms of quality, so they won't be embarrassed to assign it. I do think you'll see Chandler and Hammet on more syllabuses than Leonard.

2

Michael Brandt

After graduating from Baylor University with a BBA and earning Master of Arts in Communication Studies, Michael Brandt went to work in the film industry. He worked first for Quentin Tarantino's A Band Apart Films, where he served as both production manager and assistant editor on the Sarah Kelly documentary *Full Tilt Boogie* (1997) and as assistant editor on comedian Julia Sweeney's stand-up special, *God Said, "Ha!"* (1998). Brandt also worked as a production assistant on the Robert Rodriguez horror film, *The Faculty* (1998). During this period, Brandt and writing partner, Derek Haas, whom he'd met at Baylor, sold their first spec screenplay, *The Courier* (which would not be produced until 2013).

After having established themselves with their first script sale, Brandt and Haas then co-wrote the 2001 telefilm *Invincible*. The duo's next job would be a huge one, writing the John Singleton-helmed *2 Fast 2 Furious* (2003), which earned more than $236 million worldwide. After that, Brandt and Haas were tapped to write the screenplay for the 2007 remake of the 1957 Elmore Leonard adaptation, *3:10 to Yuma*. The film was a success, opening at number one at the box office and receiving critical acclaim.

Brandt and Haas next adapted the graphic novel *Wanted* (2004), which proved to be another colossal hit. Brandt then made his directorial debut in 2011 with *The Double*, based on his and Haas's original screenplay. Brandt and Haas then created and produced the NBC series *Chicago Justice*, *Chicago P.D.*, *Chicago Med*, and *Chicago Fire*.

Brandt was kind enough to be interviewed for this book, discussing his and Haas's (James Mangold-directed) remake of *3:10 to Yuma*, the original Halstead Welles-adapted 1957 film, and the 1953 Elmore Leonard short story that inspired both films.

ANDREW J. RAUSCH: *Had you read any of Elmore Leonard's work prior to becoming involved with* 3:10 to Yuma? *I'd read that you were primarily a fan of spy novels but I wondered if you had read Leonard.*

Perspectives on Elmore Leonard

MICHAEL BRANDT: I was definitely a fan of spy novels early on, but I read a lot of different things. I had definitely read *Get Shorty* (1990). I had read some of his quirkier, more modern novels. I had seen the original *3:10 to Yuma* (1957), but I hadn't read the short story when James Mangold first approached Derek and I about doing the film. But I had read a bunch of other Western short stories. That doesn't necessarily have anything to do with your interview. [Laughs.] You know, Louis L'Amour and guys like that, who still wrote in the 1950s at the same time Leonard was writing his. I was a huge fan of Westerns, but I hadn't read that particular story.

You said James Mangold approached you. Would you talk a little bit about the process of how you became involved and how the film got rolling?

MB: Sony had the rights at the time, and Mangold had been talking to Sony about remaking the 1957 version. Sony wasn't fully onboard, and the reason was because Westerns hadn't done all that well. I mean, really, if you look back now, this movie was something like the third biggest Western of all time after *Tombstone* (1993) and maybe *Unforgiven* (1992). Maybe not even *Unforgiven*. But it still only made seven million dollars overseas. They just don't make any money overseas. So, Sony wasn't really into it. And at the time, Derek and I had really only written the second *Fast and the Furious* movie. So Mangold's thinking was, what if I can present to the studio some guys who wrote the movie that just made over $400 million? He thought it would appeal to a younger audience and maybe make them not scared of it being a dusty old Western. He also wanted to incorporate some modern themes into it.

That's how it came together. I'd always been a fan of Jim's. He'd made so many great smaller movies. He had yet to make his bigger, giant movies. Certainly he hadn't done *The Wolverine* (2013) or any of that stuff yet. But his smaller movies were great. I always thought *Cop Land* (1997) was amazing. When the idea came around of Mangold doing *Yuma*, I was like, "Yes! 100 percent!" We then dove back into the original, and of course read Elmore's short story at that point, too. And thus began the conversations with Jim and Sony about what a modern remake would look like. It's funny, but the thing that struck me about the first movie—not the short story—there's kind of a hint of Dan Evans, which is not the same name as the guy in the short story, and he's got these kids.... He kind of limped around, and just the way he was cast— it was Van Heflin, and he sort of seemed like he was on his way out as a character. He didn't seem like that vital of a character. I thought that was interesting, and I also thought that was an opportunity in that the kids, meaning the oldest son, was not around in the movie once Dan takes off from the ranch with Ben Wade. There were two things that struck me that were a reason to make a remake. It's like, I don't know why you would ever remake *Psycho* (1960), but I can see why you would remake the original *3:10 to Yuma*. It actually feels like a TV movie. It's really only got two acts. They took Elmore's story and they kind of slapped on a setup, and then there was the movie. It didn't really have your typical three-act structure. It also didn't have that real kind of emotional ride, even though at the end, yes, it rains, and there's the wife standing in the rain as the train pulls away. It's a little silly. Even though it was great for its time, it was kind of missing something. Really when you look back, it was missing a second act.

The pitch to Sony was.... I don't know how old you are, but in the nineties we had a commercial with Michael Jordan and there were a bunch of kids singing "I wanna be like Mike, I wanna be like Mike...." And then Charles Barkley came out with a commercial where he just looked at the camera and said, "I am not a role model. Parents are role models." It was like the anti–Jordan message. And I said, "That's the movie!" That was my pitch to Sony: "That's the movie." Whether it's Allen Iverson or Charles Barkley or Michael Jordan or whoever—pick your guy in the nineties and 2000s.... Parents are still having to deal with the same things that Dan Evans would have to deal with regarding his son. His son was looking up to a guy because the guy was enigmatic and kind of an unknown quantity and basically a badass. Meanwhile, the father was missing a leg from the Civil War and couldn't pay his bills, and his son looked at him like he was a loser. While unfair, that's probably similar to every father that has boys who love the NBA today. Dad works wherever he works, but he's not playing in the NBA, so it's always a struggle for kids' attention.

Dad is never glamorous. Even if you're someone who is glamorous to other people, you're still not going to seem glamorous to your own kids.

MB: Yeah. So my pitch to Sony was that Barkley commercial. "That's the movie. We need a second act where the kid goes on the journey, and they don't even know the kid's on the journey. We can even set up a moment where the kid kind of saves the day at the very beginning, and now he's got to go along with them. Some version of some events where stuff goes down and now he's got to go with them." And that was exactly what they wanted to hear because no, we're not going to just do this walk down Main Street kind of Western. The kid's going to be in the middle of it, and it turned out to be Logan Lerman, who is such a good actor. And we're off and running at that point.

And originally it was supposed to be Tom Cruise to play Ben Wade and Eric Bana to play Dan Evans. Those were the guys who were attached. And that was about the time that Tom Cruise had that Oprah couch moment where he got on her couch and was jumping up and down. Sony, at that moment, said they didn't want to make the movie with him. So, thankfully, Russell Crowe came on right away. At that point, the script was written and we were kind of getting ready to make it. But Russell came on, and then Christian Bale came on, so we didn't really skip a beat after all that.

That cast is amazing. Especially Ben Foster. You've got two great, big-name actors in Bale and Crowe, and then Ben Foster comes on and steals every scene he's in. And frankly, I think he does that in just about every film he makes.

MB: If you read the story, even if you look at our original draft, Charlie Prince was the big tough guy. And you think of him as the big tough guy. Again, leave it Mangold to cast Ben Foster, who was like, "No, I'm going to be super dapper. I'm going to wear a double-breasted leather jacket. I'm going to play it almost like it's a love affair between me and the boss." He's such an amazing actor to even conceptualize that character in the West, because it certainly didn't follow along the genre lines. That was 100 percent Ben. If you look at the original script, he didn't look at his boss sideways like "given the chance I might kiss you." [Laughs.] That was Ben. And that's why Ben is so interesting, and that's why he does steal every scene—because he does something that is the opposite of what you think he's going to do.

I wanted to talk about the evolution of the story a little bit. You touched on this some, but I find the evolution fascinating. The original short story is really only a one-act story. It's the third act and that's it. Okay, then the Halstead Welles script for the 1957 version comes in, and it's sort of two acts now. You've got the first act and you've got the third act. Then Derek Haas and yourself come in with your version and you write a second act, which is the journey. I suppose this is blasphemous to Elmore Leonard to say this, but I feel like every version of the story gets better and a little more layered.

2. Michael Brandt

MB: Thank you for saying that, and I would agree. I think that's why it was ripe for a remake—because it didn't have a second act. You know, Elmore Leonard was paid $90 to write that story. It's what? Fifteen pages? And it's just a very sharp idea: what's the price of a man? Two guys in a hotel room. One guy needs money and one guy has money but doesn't have freedom, so what's the price? The thing about Elmore's story is that every inch of it holds up. If you look at both versions of the movie, not a lot has changed in the third act. We can get to the end of my version of *Yuma*, because definitely that changes, but in terms of conversations in the room, in terms of the brother showing up, in terms of getting him out the door and Charlie Prince showing up and here's the gang and all of that, that's Elmore's. That really hasn't changed. And it didn't need to. It's just kind of been added on.

I was lucky enough to get to spend a couple of days with Elmore before he died. This was after the movie was made. I was making another movie in Detroit, where Elmore lived. And he came by the set one day. I actually think his son brought him by. This was ten, twelve years ago. He came by the set, and then he invited us to his house. So Derek and I went out to his house, which is the most unsuspecting house. You're like, "You mean one of the greatest living writers lives in this house?" We went in, and it was just Elmore sitting by himself at the kitchen table. He was watching the Tigers on TV. He never missed a Tigers game. So we sat there for like three hours and watched the baseball game with him.

He wrote everything out longhand. He had these yellow legal pads, and he wrote everything out with this red pen. The papers were just spread out everywhere on the kitchen table. It looked like a movie set, like if you were going to set up an Elmore Leonard movie set, that's what it would be. And he had about ten beers and smoked about a hundred cigarettes in the course of the game. And he was great! He was such a character. He was exactly the character you wanted him to be. And sharp as a tack.

We talked about the ending of the movie. He very graciously signed a copy of the *Yuma* script for me that says, "A great one until the end." [Laughs.] And the reason I'm proud of that is because I actually didn't agree with the way our version of *Yuma* ended. The original script didn't end with Dan Evans dying, and it definitely didn't end with Ben Wade getting on the train himself and then whistling after his horse to follow him. Jim Mangold really felt strongly about Dan dying. I never was onboard with it, but he's the director and it's his movie, so that's what happened.

I didn't necessarily agree with the way the first one ended either. I didn't agree with the wife being out there and watching them all ride past her. That was a little campy. And then it just magically starts to rain.

I'm not speaking out of school. If Mangold was on this call, I would say this. He's heard me say this. When you add the son into the journey, when you add the son into the second act, I feel like it's such a bummer for the audience. It's one thing to have a tragic ending, but it's another thing to have a tragic ending where the son is standing there watching it happen. I just thought it was too much. I just thought, in 1880 or whatever year that takes place, a healthy husband, even one with a wooden leg, who's trying to teach his son a lesson, is better than a dead husband who did teach his son a lesson but is now dead. And the older I've gotten, the more I've kind of come to understand why Mangold wanted to end it that way. Because it does make sense in terms of my original idea of the Charles Barkley message that parents are role models. Dan Evans was the ultimate role model. But I just thought it was a bummer. I wanted Dan and Ben on that train together going to Yuma, and then Ben saying, "I've broken out of Yuma before." They did it, and they did it together. I thought it was a little harsh killing Dan at the end.

And Elmore agreed. That's why he said it was a great one until the end. That's the only reason I feel okay about that signature, because it wasn't my idea! [Laughs.] And I didn't agree with it either.

My thought about Mangold's ending is that Dan dying negates everything that Ben Wade has done. The sacrifice of himself that he makes for Dan is totally negated.
    MB: I could not agree more.

Frankly, I don't understand why Ben Wade would go ahead and get on the train after Dan is dead. If he's doing all of this in service of Dan, his getting on the train at that point seems silly.
    MB: I feel like there's a lot of having cake and trying to eat it too there. As soon as they leave the hotel room, and the first time Dan realizes Ben is actually with him and is going to help him get to the train, even though at any point he could just drop down and it's over, but he doesn't, he's helping him and kind of showing him how to get there.... It's great—I think it's the best part of the movie—when Charlie, played by Ben, realizes this. "What's Boss doing?" That's the best point in the movie, and you're right, it does negate it. It negates all of that to have

26

Dan die and Ben just put himself on the train. Which I get in theory. It's a thematic move, but then he calls to the horse, so it's just one thing after another. It's like this pendulum, and I just feel it goes back and forth too much.

I've always sort of joked about both versions of the film (and the story too), and I'm sure this is a thought you've had before. Dan could have avoided a lot of headaches if he had just taken Ben to the rail house to start with. Then they wouldn't have had to go across town. That always made me laugh. Realistically they would just surround it and blow him to pieces, and then you wouldn't have a movie.

MB: [Laughs.] Well, yeah, I guess there are a lot of ways. You could have just hung him in the middle of town in the beginning too.

One of the things you guys did that I really feel is brilliant and makes a lot of sense but wasn't in the story or the first movie is when Charlie calls the townsfolk to get involved. I think that just adds a tremendous punch to the scene.

MB: I remember when we started talking about the geography with Jim, what made it really interesting was finding out that the town was going to be pretty small, and these guys are on a second floor. They're *right there.* The window is right over Main Street, so you can have conversations. I think when we realized what the geography was going to be, we got the idea of Charlie Prince telling the townsfolk they get money for whoever shoots him. It's horrifying, but it's even more scary that Dan is up there listening to this. That was the point. It was the geography that kind of drove that. It was a pretty good idea, and honestly I don't remember whose idea it was. But I remember the geography being the thing that brought that about.

There were things in the early drafts of our script that didn't make it just for budgetary reasons. But the town was painted darker in terms of the characters that were there, than in any other version. It was because, as we did research on the railroad—When you start to write something like a Western ... the only thing I know about Westerns is what I've already seen in other Westerns. I don't have firsthand knowledge of what it was like to be there. So, you have to be careful not to write tropes you've been watching your whole life. Sometimes it's great, and sometimes you use them—the idea of genre is very important—and you use them to your advantage. And sometimes you can twist on it a little bit and use that to your advantage. But there was a book by Stephen

Ambrose about the railroads. I remember reading that, and that's also what led to the whole Chinese village. But I learned that if you got on a train in Chicago, the farther the line went—and it wasn't done yet, because it had just gotten to Contention—the shadier the people were. At some point you're going to get to the end, and that's where the workers and the whores are going to be. That was the way it was described. That was something I had never seen in a Western before. So we actually had this opening sequence where you saw a guy get on the train—I think it was in Omaha—and he started going west, and each stop got shadier and shadier. It was kind of like an opening title sequence.

Even though that didn't make it into the movie, that led to the people being pretty shady by the time they got to Contention. Because it got shadier and shadier the farther west you got, the idea that Charlie Prince could stand out in the middle of town and say, "I'm going to give money to whoever wants to kill Dan Evans" makes sense. You're going to have people stand up and say, "Yeah, that sounds good." Because they were fairly desperate. That probably wouldn't happen in Chicago or Omaha or Kansas City, but it would here, and that all came out of doing the research.

One thing I loved that I had never seen in another film was the fortified stagecoach with a Gatling gun carrying the Pinkertons. I've seen Gatling guns in other things, such as The Outlaw Josey Wales *(1976), but never like this. And I loved that you guys took what was a very average stagecoach robbery scene and added a whole other level to it.*

MB: It was just the idea of a Brinks truck and the idea that the railroad wouldn't just send their money down on any old stagecoach. It was just an idea to be different and brash and cool and again, any time you could break or bend the genre a little bit without offending people, that was the choice. I think that goes back to the original idea of Sony's, which was it can't be a dusty old western. Okay, where do we start? Let's start with an armored car. We haven't seen that before in the old west. It was that kind of.... I'm not saying it was a *Fast & Furious* thing, but it was that kind of mentality where it was, "Okay, how do we put things on steroids here?" That was to make the studio happy and also because it looked cool.

When the film came out and you guys were doing press, all of the interviewers remarked about how different the film was from your previous film, 2 Fast 2 Furious. *It seems to me that they aren't really all that different. I see your version of* 3:10 to Yuma *as being an action movie set in the old west. Do you think that's accurate?*

MB: That was a definite early goal. It was a goal, not to make it an action movie in the sense of ... we weren't going to give up character to make it an action movie. But the best action movies still have as much characterization as the best westerns. We definitely wanted to impose a little testosterone into it in general. We knew what the marching orders were from the studio, and Jim, too. *Yuma* would always go back and lean on how the son looked at his father and how he looked at Ben Wade. We would always go back to that. *Fast & Furious*, every movie, and this is why they're successful, it always goes back to, "We're a family. How are we going to get through this?" Whether you had Vin Diesel.... We didn't have Vin Diesel in ours, so when they couldn't make a deal with Vin, our next thought was, "We've got to create a new character who's an old friend of Paul Walker's, because the theme of family still has to be there." If you just consistently fall back on that, you can't go wrong.

I'm not sure where *Yuma* and *Fast & Furious* would crossover other than you had two guys writing them at a time in their life when they just thought those things were really cool, so that's what they did. And that's what Derek and I were doing.

The last time I watched the original film, it struck me for the first time that Halstead Welles, likely at the behest of the producers, really adapted the story into a play on High Noon *(1952). Both are about men whom no one really comes forward to help, who have to wait until a pre-specified moment of action that the whole film is built around and may well result in their death, and in both cases the protagonist has the opportunity to walk away but stay primarily because their principles won't allow them to leave.*

MB: I didn't think of it that way, but you're definitely right.

I think part of it is that both of them have time in the title, so you can't do anything until that time comes, whether it's noon or 3:10. [Laughs.] A different way to look at it is that that is what happens when you don't have cell phones. Back then, everything was about time. Something happened at a certain time, and everybody knew it hap-pened at that time, and you couldn't let anyone know if it wasn't hap-pening at that time. You know what I mean? You kind of had to set a time because you couldn't call anybody. So it was like, "Hey, we're going to take them there and get on this train or whatever, and that's going to take us three days." But it was all about time, not about communication. So I think there's something to do with that. Certainly *High Noon* gets all the credit. Walking the guy down Main Street at a certain time is a bit of a genre trope, and Halstead leaned into that, and that's great. But so did Elmore, obviously, too.

I hadn't thought about that comparison, but I will tell you that when you're writing a movie that's set in the 1800s, just the idea that one character can't call another character is, at times, so frustrating, and at other times it's the most freeing thing in the world that you don't have to deal with cell phones. And time was much more of a factor.

I want to bring up another thing I really like about your version of 3:10 to Yuma. Aside from the addition of the journey to Contention, you've also got the Apache attack. I feel that those things give Dan and Ben time to develop a more realistic bond. I sort of always felt that aspect was lacking a bit in the original film, making the ending slightly more difficult to buy into. I wondered if you wanted to talk a little bit about the addition of those elements.

MB: In Halstead's version, there wasn't an Indian attack, right?

There wasn't an attack. There wasn't really even a trip. They just go from point A straight to point B.

MB: Right. There's just kind of a cut from, "Okay, we've got him" to Contention. I think the Apache attack was a leftover from my watching *The Outlaw Josey Wales* as a child. Characters came and went in and out of Josey Wales' life as he's on his journey. The Indians just scared the hell out of me. The idea of Indians as shadows, to me, was always just a scary thing. The fact that they could just be there, but they're not there. You didn't know they were there, but they were. That, to me, is just scary. It was really that. I felt like Indians in Westerns have kind of fallen by the wayside. Maybe for good reason. Maybe in today's world you write a different version of it. But just the idea that you have to go through an area that's just scary as hell.... And remember, we had to manufacture a second act. We had to create a journey. They had to go *somewhere*, and part of that journey was the Chinese railroad camp, which was a real thing. And then also, what other kinds of things are they going to run into along the way? And having to take a turn and go through a place that you know you're not supposed to go through is, to me, just scary. Also, it's a little bit of a nod to *The Warriors* (1979) or *Escape from New York* (1981), where you don't want to go through the Bronx at this time of night, but you have to. That stuff has always scared the hell out of me, so I think that's kind of where that came from.

Let's talk about the ending to all three incarnations of the story. It's clear that Ben Wade admires Dan by the time we get to the end of the story. In your mind, what is it that Ben sees in him that allows him to basically sacrifice himself and his men to aid him?

MB: I can only speak on my version. I'm not sure about the others. Like in Elmore's version, for instance. In Elmore's original story, Dan still forces him on the train. Ben helps him a little bit, but really, they don't have the showdown with Charlie. They have a bit of one, but it's really just him getting a couple of shots off before Dan forces him onto the train.

I think Halstead, to his credit, fell into the idea even more so than Elmore, if you ask me, that Ben's level of respect would be such that "I'm going to get on the train for him." Or "with him." Which I thought was amazing.

I think, in ours, it really goes back to Ben Wade sitting at the dinner table with the family. And he meets the wife. He starts to talk a little bit out of turn, and then he stops. Then here are the kids, and the kids actually put him in his place. "We don't talk that way" and "we say grace...."

I don't necessarily agree also with our version with Ben killing all his guys. But he does it because he realizes that he's been running with animals. They are fucking animals. And he only knows that because of the time he just spent, starting with Dan's family, and then with Dan and his son throughout this. Then he looks at his gang at the end and realizes they really are animals. Early on, it's apparent that he's put himself on a pedestal in his own head, but I think by the time he's gone through this and he gets to the end, he looks at his guys and sees that they're no better than the piles of dirt around, because they're just there for the money and to get drunk and that's it. I don't think he wants to be associated with that anymore. So, I think that level of respect just comes from him what it would be like if Allen Iverson or someone like that spent a week with a father and his son. It starts with the son saying, "I don't like my dad," and by the end, Allen Iverson is like, "Dude, your dad is the greatest." [Laughs.]

Ben Wade eventually assisting Dan is one of the real charms of both film versions. This may be a silly question, but I was wondering, do you think that could really happen? Do you think it's believable?

31

MB: [Laughs.] I will say that's the beauty of movies. That's why we watch them, right? That's why you do it, because you get to watch a guy who's played Gladiator and every badass under the sun, turn to a guy who's got one leg and say, "I'm doing this with you. We're doing this together. That's it."

I mean, would a guy cut his corn in Iowa? No, but *Field of Dreams* (1989) is my favorite movie ever. So can I explain it? No. But do I love it? Fuck yeah. I'm going to watch it every time it's on TV.

That's one of the joys of writing screenplays or novels—you're creating the world and its boundaries. As such, anything can happen as long as it makes sense to the world of the particular piece.

MB: One hundred percent. The more seasoned I get as a writer, the more I realize that that is to be embraced and also be relished. *Fast & Furious* can set its own rules because it's just breaking physics. It's like, "Oh, that car could never get over that bridge." But who cares? That's setting physical rules. And I think the more seasoned I become as a writer, it's the emotional rules where you just allow for things. Would that person ever do that? Well, yeah, he would, because I've paved enough road and he's driven on that road long enough that now he will make that choice.

You can never really predict what a person will do in real life anyway. You hear people say, "This character would never really do this." But you can't know that. Every person you know has, at one point or another, made a decision you would never have expected them to make. So why would movie characters be any different?

MB: Right. But also, that can be a legitimate complaint against a character's decision. And that can just be the fault of the writer not having paved enough road. It's not earned. I do think that it's earned that, by the time Dan and Wade get out of that hotel room, my favorite moment when Ben turns on Charlie. He doesn't kill him, but Charlie realizes something is happening. He's like, "Boss? Boss, what are you doing?" That is earned. We've just spent an hour-and-a-half earning that moment. That's why I love that moment so much. But Charlie Prince wasn't on that ride. That's why he doesn't know it. That's why it's such a fun moment, because he's as surprised as anybody. But we were on that ride, so that moment got earned. That's why I love it so much. You get to watch another character having to deal with something that we were privy to.

2. Michael Brandt

What are some other Elmore Leonard adaptations that you like, and maybe why?

MB: Certainly for me, *Out of Sight* is my number one. I think everyone has to start with that and *Get Shorty*, both of which were adapted by Scott Frank. I'm definitely a *Justified* fan.

Remind me, what other ones am I missing?

Most people list Jackie Brown.

MB: You know what's funny is, I used to work for Quentin [Tarantino]. I was an assistant editor for Quentin. He was prepping *Jackie Brown* when I was working for him. I didn't actually work on *Jackie Brown*, I was working on another movie he was producing.

But it's not my favorite, and I have a very specific reason why. Even though Quentin is my favorite filmmaker. I think he's the most interesting filmmaker of my lifetime, and *Jackie Brown* is to me.... I hate to say it, but I think it's the most flawed of all his films, and for one very simple reason: they hatch a plan, then the plan works, and the movie is over.

I will admit, I haven't read Elmore's version, but it was really surprising to me. And this was while I was working with Quentin that I got a copy of the script, which was about a year before it was finished. I just kept reading it and waiting, like "When's that Quentin thing gonna happen?" When's that *whammo!*? [Laughs.] And it doesn't. It never happens. So that, to me, should have been a match made in heaven, but it just wasn't. I think that's why it's so curious.

A lot of times when people talk about the great Elmore Leonard film adaptations, they talk about the ones we just mentioned. But very rarely does your version of 3:10 to Yuma *get mentioned, and I do think it belongs up there in that upper echelon. I do, very sincerely, believe it's up there with those films. Why do you think that is? Do you think it's because it's a Western and not a crime film, or do you think it's because it's such an expansion beyond his original story?*

MB: I don't think, in general, people think of it as an Elmore Leonard movie.

I did find it interesting that the promotional materials and ads for the film never played up his involvement. I thought maybe it was because people only associate him with crime.

MB: Crime and wacky characters. But also, if you think about the ones that are the most highly regarded, they are full Elmore Leonard stories from beginning to end. They're not just a short story that's been expanded over the years.

I'm Googling Elmore Leonard adaptations and their rankings right now. According to IndieWire, we're the fifth. *Get Shorty* is fourth. *Hombre* (1967) is three, which I'll admit I've never seen. *Jackie Brown* is two, so it's already lost me. And *Out of Sight* is one.

You know, our film was based on a short story and another movie, so I think that waters it down in people's minds. "Is it really Elmore Leonard?" Which it wholeheartedly is. I mean, everything is centered on that conversation in the hotel.

3

Paul Challen

Dundas, Ontario, author Paul Challen has written more than 60 books on a wide variety of subjects, including sports, history, popular culture, and science, for children and adult readers. In 2000, he wrote a biography of Elmore Leonard titled *Get Dutch!* According to Challen, his aim in writing the book was "to provide Leonard lovers with a biography of his life and work from the perspective of a fellow fan, while incorporating insights from those who collaborated with the crime fiction legend, including agents, editors, screen adapters, and his full-time researcher—through firsthand interviews, research at Leonard's archives at the University of Detroit, and discussions with academic and literary critics, for a well-rounded portrait of the man and author."

In addition to *Get Dutch!*, Challen has written books on NBA legend Isiah Thomas and actor Hugh Laurie, as well as an in-depth look at the television series, *The West Wing.* He has also contributed to a variety of publications including the *Toronto Star, National Post, Hamilton Spectator, Toronto Life*, and *Quill & Quire.* He also teaches writing at the University of Waterloo, and has worked full-time as an editor for several book and magazine publishing companies, and in private-sector and government communications and policy departments.

ANDREW J. RAUSCH: *How did you first discover Elmore Leonard's work?*

PAUL CHALLEN: I first discovered Elmore Leonard through film, to be honest. I think it was *Get Shorty* (1995) that was the first movie I saw of Leonard's. That was the first inkling I had that Leonard existed. That would've come out in 1995. He'd been writing a lot before that, and when I had seen this film I asked a friend of mine if he had seen it, and he said, "Yeah. Did you know that was based on a book by this guy called Elmore Leonard? You should check him out!"

I worked in a library at the time, so this colleague and I talked about books all the time. He'd recommend a ton of books. I think the next one that he recommended I look at was *Freaky Deaky* (1988). So I read that and was absolutely hooked! I think at some point after that, I saw *Out of Sight* (1998), the George Clooney and Jennifer Lopez movie. I was really into that as well. I think, like a lot of people, what really kept me going was the movies and not the books.

What were your initial thoughts on the first couple of books you read? What stood out to you?

PC: I had never read anything that was that heavy in dialogue, other than maybe a comic book. As I learned from Scott Frank as I was doing the research on my book, there are entire pages of *Get Shorty* that basically appear on the screen. It comes from that old adage, "If it's not on the page, it's not on the stage." That's one of the things Frank talked about. He's often asked the secret to adapting Leonard novels into great movies, because there were so many failures before that. It wasn't rocket science. They were all right there in the book! He basically told me, "I just pulled the dialogue out and put it into the screenplay."

I think that's what really struck me. I hadn't read any dialogue that read like that. That was kind of very representative of the way that people actually speak. It was like nothing I had read. Leonard captured that somehow in a way I had never seen before. He had all those rules for writing. A big one was something like "don't, as an author, describe stuff when you could have a character describe it for you." Instead of the author saying "it's scorching hot, you could fry an egg on the pavement," he'd just have a character say that. I thought, boy, this is a really refreshing way of writing! In a way, it sort of took the authorial heavy-handedness, which at that stage in my life I was starting to hate, and put it all in the voices of the characters. I suppose it wasn't technical. After all, the characters are being told to talk by the author. But the author is not in there as much as the characters. I think I saw that [as] really, really appealing.

In addition to all that was the fact that these characters were not like ones I had ever met before. The Chili Palmer character in *Get Shorty*, which I later learned was researched by his full-time paid researcher, Greg Sutter. I realized I had never met a character like that before. There was something about Chili Palmer in the book and later in the movie that just seemed authentic. I wouldn't actually know what authentic means because I had never really met a loan shark, but it had that ring to it, you know?

3. *Paul Challen*

Sometimes I wonder, are they authentic or do they just have the appearance of being authentic? I wonder if it's as authentic as we think it is. For instance, when we talk about Leonard writing dialogue the way people actually talk, it's a heightened, stylized version of that, because in truth, most people speak in a way that is much more boring than Leonard characters. Because of that, I wonder if his characters are that way, as well. I would imagine his characters are a lot more interesting than the guy who robs the liquor store down the street from you.

PC: Well, somebody pointed that out about the character in *Be Cool* (1990), Joe Loop. The movie *Be Cool* (2005), by the way, is the worst abomination of anything ever related to Leonard of all time. An absolutely terrible sequel—the movie, that is—to *Get Shorty*. Which I can certainly say on record! At least they got the character Joe Loop kind of correct. Somebody pointed this out to me. He's a guy breaking people's legs for a living. He's not a very nice guy. And he probably does read with his mouth open. Remember in the movie, and it was described in the book, the first time he'd ever eaten what he called Jew food. He'd never been to a deli and he had slobber all over his mouth. "Hey, this is pretty good!" And he ends up getting the daylights beaten out of him by the character The Rock plays in the movie, but my point is, those guys probably are unsavory and not as stylized as they are in movies, right?

On a similar note, I see a lot of crime writers who are trying to write authentic characters get criticized for having characters that aren't politically correct. I think it's unrealistic to imagine a lot of lowlife characters having sophisticated, politically correct, liberal views.

PC: Yeah. He murders people, but he collects 16th-century artwork on the side. It's not going to happen! It's an interesting question, what Greg Sutter brought to that whole enterprise because, from my understanding talking to Sutter for a brief time, he was hired to go down to Palm Beach, I think it was, and do a bunch of research on bail bondsmen so he could get that Max Cherry character down pat for the book *Rum Punch* (1992), which was later made into the movie *Jackie Brown* (1997). He talked to bail bondsmen, he photographed them, he did up a big dossier on them, he interviewed them on tape, and he put together a whole portrait for Leonard to draw on for what he was ultimately like. To the point you were making, he just seemed like a guy who would be a bail bondsman, but I have no way of knowing that as a guy living up here in Canada.

There's another author I like, Alan Furst. He writes World War II spy novels. His books are all set in World War II, they're all spies in these European countries during World War II. The word on him is that if he describes something, like a street scene in Warsaw with gas lamps or whatever, then that actually happened. He's a dedicated researcher. You can bank on the fact it actually happened. But you have to remember, this is all fiction. I'm not trying to cross-check with anything that happened in historical records. And the guy's trying to tell a really cool story, and he takes a lot of satisfaction in the research he does, but at the end of the day, okay, so ... it's all true. *So what?* But that's the thing that always struck me about Leonard. The whole accuracy and verisimilitude and the amount of detail. Is it for the reader? Is it really just for the writer? Is it a weird conversation we're having around accuracy and how that adds to the storytelling capabilities? It's a really interesting point.

You decided to write Get Dutch *in 1998 after seeing* Out of Sight. *What made you decide Leonard might be a good subject for a book?*

PC: My first book was an exercise in failure to actually to try to interview my subject. It was about the basketball player turned into general manager of the Toronto Raptors, Isiah Thomas. I went through a really frustrating exercise of trying to interview him. Then his agent accepted, and then Thomas never actually did any of the interviews. I ultimately published the book without his help. I worked with the same publisher on the second book, and we came to an agreement. I said, "This isn't really what I want to do." And they said, "This isn't really what we want to publish unless you actually get an interview with Leonard."

Part of it was purely just wanting to meet the guy. Wanting to know a bit more about how he put his craft together. I think the thing that was really compelling to me was that when I found out was that for his first three decades as a writer he wasn't doing it full time, which is something I related to personally. I was writing on the side, late at night after my kids went to bed, or early in the morning before I was going off to work. So I thought that was kind of interesting. I admired all that in Leonard and I wanted to see how he did it and how he did it really successfully. Then, when I looked into his body of work and how he changed genres from a Western writer to a crime writer, I thought, that's really interesting, too. And then I looked at how many books he had written before he actually made any money. I thought, this guy's a professional. He cranks it out. He does it as a side job. It seems really interesting. He doesn't live that far from me in Detroit, so I could probably drive and meet the guy. Then it turned out that he was coming to Toronto on a book tour, so I ended up getting an interview with him and it worked out really well.

3. Paul Challen

I wondered, though, how many people were going to buy a book about the life of a writer. I knew I wasn't going to sell a lot of books, and the publisher was like, "Yeah, we're not really sure. People love to read his books, but how many want to read about him?" I had to kind of get this compelling story about how many people were going to buy it. I think the final thing that stirred the publisher was back to the movie thing. More and more people were starting to learn about Leonard as a writer.

I understand the first time you reached out to Leonard, he politely blew you off.

PC: Well, I was kind of used to it. I had done a fair bit of journalism up to that point. I was kind of prepared for it and used to people not being that willing to talk to you. As I mention in the book, I did kind of a sneaky thing. I knew a publicist and Leonard was going to Toronto to do a reading. I went to a newspaper I had written some profiles for before and said, "If I can get down to Toronto and get an interview with this guy, would you be interested in running a profile?" They said yes. So I set this up with the publicist, and they said, "If you can get a twenty minute interview with this guy, we'll do the book." And we ended up talking for an hour and fifteen minutes. He was really nice. The newspaper published the profile. He had just come out with *Be Cool*. Then I sent him the profile and said, "I'm not sure if you connected the dots, but I was the guy who had initially come to you about writing the book. And then that was me interviewing you, and here's the profile I wrote. So I guess you read it and you can see that I'm not a completely clueless guy." [Laughs.] So he said, "Okay, I'll do it, but I can't talk to you for another six months," or something like that. He said, "I'm down in Florida working away on my next book. Come back to me in six months." I think it was six months. It was a fairly long amount of time like that.

So then I started reading all of his books like crazy and did as much research as I could, so when I came back to him I would be really well-prepared to speak to him. That actually turned out pretty well. He put me into contact with Scott Frank and his publisher and his editor and his archives. My only regret, and you'll automatically know this, is that I should have gotten him to give me, because I'm fully confident he would have, Quentin Tarantino's phone number. He would have given it to me, I just didn't have the guts to ask for it. But I should have. I am also positive Tarantino would have spoken to me about his connection with Leonard! But Leonard was really, really helpful. He never asked for any kind of final say on the manuscript or anything. He never authorized anything. I was free to sort of talk to everyone I could talk to and then write whatever I wanted to write. And then I remember he signed an advanced reading copy of *Pagan Babies* (2013), which I still have. The inscription said something like, "To Paul, my biographer. Trusting you." [Laughs.] It was basically him saying, "Don't write any stupid shit in your book about me!"

Then when the book came out, I think he liked it and we went for a meal the next time he was in Toronto. Had a nice chat. He said it was the first time he'd ever gone for sushi, which I find hard to believe. [Laughs.] The book was reviewed in Detroit and Toronto and all these places, and the critics quite rightly pointed out that I was not very critical at all. For instance, one review said I should have addressed his alcoholism a lot more directly. People said it was a typical book written by a fan who's not being critical at all and is just fawning over all of his work. That's probably true, but it was only the second book I'd ever written and I was pretty young. I was in my early thirties, I think. If you're in Canada, just getting a book reviewed in the *Toronto Star* was great for me. It didn't matter whether or not these reviewers, some of whom came off sounding kind of pompous, to be honest, actually liked it or not.

Your interview with Leonard in Toronto at the King Edward Hotel was an interesting situation because he was doing other things while you spoke. Would you like to talk about that?

PC: He was signing books and I was passing them over to him. He was doing the early version of multi-tasking, I guess. He was like, "I've got this big stack I've got to sign. Would you pass them over to me as I sign them?" But I don't feel like that compromised his answers. I've been in situations like that where you're talking to someone and they're like, "Oh, man, I'm dying for a smoke. Do you mind if we go outside and you can interview me there?" That kind of stuff.

Let me put it this way, I've heard him say a lot of the same stuff in different interviews. I think he had kind of a standard biography he had on hand when people would ask him these things. He was ready with these same answers. My aim was to ask him at least a few questions that he had never been asked before. I'm not sure I succeeded on it, but I did want to press him a little bit on the writing from five a.m. to seven a.m. that he did in the early part of his career. You know, he'd get up and be disciplined. He wouldn't read a magazine or a book and he wouldn't make himself coffee until he had sat down and written for at least two hours. I remember asking him about that period and I'd never seen him sort of say it anywhere else, but he said, "I would not be talking to you here today if I hadn't have done that." And I thought, that's a pretty good, like a really real good way of him saying, "Busting ass all those years early in the morning has led me to a position where you're talking to me here today."

The other thing that I wanted to ask about, because I was doing a lot of work myself at the time that was very much "paying the bills" work, was his work in advertising. I was the editor of an industrial trade magazine that was about occupational health and safety. I didn't love the work at all, but I had little children and bills to pay, so I was doing trade magazine editing. The people that I worked for at the time would say, "You're learning a lot of skills that might seem to you like they're just about occupational health and safety, but you're learning a lot of other important things. You're learning how to write quickly and concisely and be part of a team," and blah, blah, blah. At the time I didn't buy it, but I certainly do now. So I said to Leonard, "Is there anything that you learned in your early years writing ad copy for the auto industry? For dealerships and pick-up trucks that helped with your fiction?" And he immediately shot back, "No. No way. Never. I didn't learn a damn thing." I was hoping he'd say, "Yes! Much like your employers are telling you, you can learn lots of valuable lessons!" But he was like, "No. I learned nothing." [Laughs.]

How do you think it happens that a mild-mannered man such as Leonard came to write about criminals and these hard-nosed characters as deftly and authentically as he did? Do you have any thoughts or theories on that?

PC: I asked him the same question. I'll never forget his answer. He looked at me point blank and said, "Well, I make 'em up!" He had this air about him like, "Well, what the hell do you think I do?" I was saying, "You're a nice guy, mild-mannered guy. You live a nice middle-class life in a suburb of Detroit and you've got a wife and a bunch of kids. You've got a nice house. What's a nebbish like you doing writing about all these bad guys?" And he just point-blank basically says, "I just use my imagination—that's what a writer does!" [Laughs.] That might be the single best answer that I got from him the whole time. That taught me that, if you can write at a certain level, as a professional, if you need to you can just about write anything. I'm sure that if I told you that I needed you to come to Toronto tomorrow and do my job for me in the Ontario provincial government, writing policy documents, I know you could do it because you're a good writer. I feel that if you have those skills, you can adapt them. It's almost like he was saying, "Hey, look, this is what I do. I put words on a page. If I need to make stuff up, I make it up!" I honestly think for him it was just that.

And as evidence, there is the whole thing with him starting off as a Western writer. When his agent told him that Westerns weren't really paying anymore, he just said, "Okay, then I'll switch." And just like that, he switched genres. Literally the next day. I found that correspondence between him and his agent in his papers at the University of Detroit. There was none of this hand-wringing angst about "I can't, because in my deep inner soul I write Westerns." None of that bullshit. He just said, "Yep, okay," and he switched.

You've stated in the past that Unknown Man No. 89 *(1977) is your favorite Elmore Leonard novel. Why is that? What aspects of that novel most resonate with you?*

PC: I don't know why I said that. Looking back on it now over distance, I'd probably say that *Get Shorty* is my favorite novel. But I still think *Unknown Man* typified the kind of unknown Leonard. It had a lot of these tropes and tricks. I'll put it this way: if you were a literary scholar who really knows how to spot this sort of thing, you'd probably see books like *Unknown Man No. 89* or *Mr. Majestyk* (1974) and go, "Yeah, this guy is gonna make it big someday." You'd kind of look at it and go, "Right—this is him before he got really big, but he's showing you all the chops that made him big."

I'm not sure why I loved *Unknown Man No. 89* so much. If I had to go back and rank now, it might not be number one, but at the time, I can remember making that statement and being pretty happy with it. I need to go back and re-read that. It's been a while since I read a lot of these novels.

You know, here's a point I should make in this interview in the context of memory and remembering characters stuff. Two quick things on that. One is that I read all the Leonard novels over that space of that six months before he agreed to do the interview and when I actually interviewed him. As a result, today, like 20 years later, they all run together in my mind like a blur of plots and characters and settings. But here is the second thing—somebody pointed out that, at the end of the day, basically all of Leonard's protagonists are essentially the same guy. So at the end of the day, it's always the same kind of understated mentally tough, not very flashy, get the job done, women love them kind of guy. It's always the same guy, right? So it's natural that that stuff would be confusing, because there's very little difference—you could argue this all day, and it would be fun to argue this—between, say, Raylan Givens and Joe LaBrava and Max Cherry and Jack Foley from *Out of Sight*. They're not the exact same characters, but they are the same basic type of guy. I read once that, unlike an author like Georges Simenson who brought Chief Inspector Maigret back for like 75 books, Leonard didn't write about the same character (at least in name) over and over, because often the rights to the characters were part of sales he made of his work to the movies. I am not sure that is true, but it seems kind of likely.

No one seems to be able to point out what the definitive Leonard novel is. And when you ask people, they can't pinpoint a specific novel. I think he was a hugely talented writer, but I think the sameness of his characters and his novels are the reason why people have a difficulty pointing to one book as being his masterwork.

PC: Paradoxically, that's why we love writers. Because they give us what we want and expect time and time again. If Stephen King were to write something under his own name that was completely different than all the other Stephen King stuff you've read, you'd be like, WTF? What's going on here? It's a weird thing that the public wants, in my opinion—they want the same thing over and over. Did you ever see the Coen Brothers movie *Barton Fink*? Where the guy says, "We need that great Barton Fink feeling. But of course, since you're Barton Fink you know that better than we do!" So we want that good, classic Elmore Leonard delivery and the tone and the dialogue and the setting. Okay, so they all kind of are the same. You can't remember if it's on a ranch or a bail bondsman or a federal marshal or a photographer or whatever they are, but we want that packaged up, not identically every time. But if he were to write something completely different from that, we wouldn't like it. And he wrote a lot of them, so it's natural that we would confuse the details.

This is all unlike another writer I love very much, the American Richard Ford. He comes out with a novel every ten years, about his favorite character, the sportswriter-turned-real-estate-salesman Frank Bascombe, so they're real sharp in my mind because I've got ten years to think about them!

When you interviewed Leonard he told you, "I think I've probably written too many books. If I had written eight books and died, I'd end up being a much bigger name than I will ever end up being now. You can't write as much as I do and still be taken seriously." What are your thoughts on that? Do you believe there's a degree of truth to that?

PC: I remember I actually asked him that question with Ford as a reference point. And I think he actually did think a lot about the whole being taken seriously thing in terms of whether or not his work was literature, whether he was a serious writer. The academy sort of always looks at Leonard in a bit of a sneering, dismissive way, and genre fiction is looked as not being serious. I asked him, "Are you going to be seen as a great American writer one day? Are people going to say, Hemingway, Faulkner, Steinbeck, and Leonard?" I think his answer was a nod to the fact that a guy that cranks out a book a year on the topics he writes about, can he really be taken seriously by the academy? I think that's what he meant. I think if he had held back and maybe only done five of them, he would have been thought of as a more serious writer. I think he was tuned in enough to actually think about that, but he did not let it ruin his life. Unlike what I have read about, for example, Simenon, who apparently was always tortured by the idea of only being valued as a "genre writer." Leonard was a pretty plain-spoken guy with a pretty solid middle-class background. But I think that was what he was reacting to. The idea of the genre fiction one-book-a-year guy and not being part of the pantheon of the more respected literary writers.

For a lot of years, he was dismissed as a genre writer. Now that the literary elite are recognizing him more, do you think they are fully embracing him or do you think they're making this admission begrudgingly?

PC: I think probably the fact that when people pass away, whether it's in music or classic arts or writers, unfortunately, it often takes them not being around anymore for them to be more appreciated. I think with what's going on with Leonard, it'll be a while. His genre isn't dead. People are still writing about crime. Whereas the baroque period in painting is kind of over. People are still making the music and still recording it, but I don't think there's a hell of a lot of baroque composers anymore. Maybe by definition, there can't be, since "baroque" has a certain time frame implied around it. But there's still that crime genre, from at least Poe and probably way earlier, that people can look at and go into the bookstore and beeline right for the mysteries. People think those books and categories aren't very serious, and Leonard's books are still there.

I think when people actually look at the metrics or the measurement of what actually makes good writing, it's becoming more and more obvious how great he was. And he didn't hurt his own cause by publishing his amazing list of rules for great writing. Knowing him, the little that I did, I don't think it was a PR move, but as a posthumous guarantor of people still talking about you and thinking about you and remembering you. You couldn't do any better than that. I've seen that quoted at corporate functions. It's all over the place. It's great. It can actually be applied to any kind of writing you could do, whether it's Westerns or fiction or whatever else. I've actually even used it in mentoring people on how to write good government documents, believe it or not.

Do you believe that Leonard will still be read in fifty to 100 years from now, and what books have the best chance of survival?

PC: Yes, I do believe that he will absolutely be read fifty to 100 years from now. I also believe some of the films based on his books will be as well. I honestly think that *Jackie Brown, Out of Sight,* and *Get Shorty* will still have a place on movie lists in fifty to 100 years as films that were well-made, well-considered, with great dialogue, and that's why they will be praised. It won't necessarily be the acting or the cinematography, but it will be Leonard's dialogue. I have a pet theory in fact that one day, *Jackie Brown* will actually be seen as Tarantino's best movie. Of course I will be long gone by then, so it's a safe bet for me to make!

As far as books, I honestly think that some of his Westerns, short stories maybe, will still be read because when people are chronicling American literature, they won't be able to chronicle it without talking about Westerns. People will talk about 19th-century, early 20th-century Westerns. They'll also talk about some of Leonard's short stories like "The Tonto Woman" (1998). I think people will remember those three films and they'll remember some of his Westerns, too. To me, those are what will keep his legacy alive in my opinion.

4

Max Allan Collins

Max Allan Collins is a two-time Shamus Award-winning author best known for the *Road to Perdition* trilogy (graphic novels and traditional novels), which served as the basis of the 2002 film starring Tom Hanks. He has also written a number of other popular series, including those about the characters Elliot Ness, Nolan, Mallory, Nathan Heller, and Quarry, which was adapted into a Cinemax series. In addition, he was tapped to complete a number of unfinished works by his friend Mickey Spillane after Spillane's 2006 death. The resulting Spillane/Collins novels include *Dead Street* (2007), *Kiss Her Goodbye* (2011), and *Kill Me, Darling* (2015), just to name a few.

Collins has written many film novelizations, including *Maverick* (1994), *Saving Private Ryan* (1998), and *American Gangster* (2007). He has also penned books based on the television series *NYPD Blue* (1993), *CSI* (2000), and *Criminal Minds* (2005). He has co-written 10 *Trash 'n' Treasure* books with his wife, Barbara. He has also written *Black Hats* (2007) and *Red Sky in Morning* (2008) under the pseudonym Patrick Culhane.

He has also done significant work in comics, having worked on everything from *Batman* (1986) to *Mickey Spillane's Mike Danger* (1995) to *Harlan Ellison's Dream Corridor* (1995). Collins' original graphic novels and series (beyond *Road to Perdition*) include *Ms. Tree's Thrilling Detective Adventures* (1983) and *Quarry's War* (2018).

In addition to all of this, Collins has also written and directed a handful of films, including the 1995 adaptation of his novel *Mommy* (1977), starring Patty MacCormack.

ANDREW J. RAUSCH: *What was the first Elmore Leonard novel you ever read?*

MAX ALLAN COLLINS: That would have been *Hombre* (1961), when I was in high school, because I liked the movie. I was not a regular reader of westerns, but remember being impressed that the style was consistent with the tough mystery fiction—[Dashiell] Hammett in particular—that had become my real literary enthusiasm by that point. Also, there was dark humor, and I was caught up in the black comedy of *Catch-22* (1961) and Kurt Vonnegut. The first crime novel of his I read was *The Big Bounce* (1969), which I liked very much—like so many Gold Medal originals, it was a take on the James M. Cain type of story, and an especially fresh one.

You told me you met Leonard once. What can you tell me about that experience?

MAC: I met Leonard at a Bouchercon very early in my career. I knew he would be there, so I took my copy of *The Big Bounce* with me. He was pleased to see that when I handed it to him to sign. He was friendly, that rare combination of self-contained confidence and approachability. We had a nice chat and I told him I was a working professional, and he was supportive. I saw him at several Edgar dinners, and he always remembered me, called me by name, and we would chat briefly. That felt good. I knew he was a major talent of his generation. The first time, when he signed my *Big Bounce* paperback, I asked him if he'd seen the film version. He said he had walked out of it, and I admitted I'd liked it. Had he seen the scene in the graveyard with Leigh Taylor-Young, and he smiled and said, "Yes, I stayed for that."

What are some things you like most about Leonard's work?

MAC: His dialogue is his strong point, and his vivid characters are another big plus. I like the toughness of his protagonists that are also tempered by humanity. When I was reading him regularly, I knew he had started in westerns and I liked the flow between the two genres, the way he brought some of each to the other.

You've told me that you're less a fan of Leonard's later work. Why is that?

MAC: First I have to explain something. I read everything Leonard did up to a point early in my career when I stopped reading much mystery and crime fiction. It happened when I had been reading George V. Higgins and his style of dialogue got into my writing and I had trouble shaking it. Somehow the influences of [Mickey] Spillane and Hammett and [Raymond] Chandler and Cain and [Ed] McBain and [Jim] Thompson and [Donald] Westlake had all come together in a way that added something that seemed my own; once I'd injected myself into the mix, anyway. I decided I was no longer a fan, but a pro, and stopped reading the competition unless I was on an awards committee or something. I kept reading McBain and the very rare Spillane publication, and for a while Don Westlake in his various forms, because he was the last really major influence on me. After a while, I even stopped reading Don. Leonard was getting more and more spare and, I have to say, mannered, and I knew he would be dangerous—that I'd find myself imitating him without meaning to. So that's a factor. I read everything through and including *52 Pickup* (1974). This was right around when I stopped reading other crime writers. Now and then I'd read a Leonard, again if I were on an awards committee or just to check in on him, because he had become not this cult-ish guy I read, but somebody major.

My feeling—and some of this comes from movie versions of his stuff, where he wrote the screenplays—was that he seemed to be starting with a premise, letting his gift for dialogue carry him into creating some interesting characters, and then just let things play out and see what happened. That's not my preference as a reader or, particularly, as a writer. I like to know where I'm heading. I like structure. I like a certain formality within which I do my improv, so to speak. And I'm not saying that's the only way. But it's my way.

You told me you wanted to discuss Leonard's 10 rules of writing.

MAC: I see writers all over the place citing Leonard's 10 rules as gospel, which is ridiculous. Leonard was too egocentric a writer for many of the rules to be of much use to anybody else. Like most writers, he developed his own "rules" based on trial and error, and his own taste. I put "rules" in quotes because I don't believe there are any—just strategies.

Leonard's first rule is to never open a book with weather. What are your thoughts on this one?

MAC: In his very first rule, Leonard lets us know how worthless his suggestions are. Ed McBain used weather all the time in his omniscient openings to 87th Precinct novels. Like this, from *The Pusher* (1956): "Winter came in like an anarchist with a bomb. Wild, shrieking, puffing hard, it caught the city in cold, froze the marrow and froze the heart. The wind roared under eaves and tore around corners, lifting hats and lifting skirts, caressing warm thighs with icy-cold fingers." Here's Chandler in "Red Wind" (1946): "There was a desert wind blowing that night." How about this from Spillane's *The Killing Man* (1989): "Some days hung over Manhattan like a huge pair of unseen pincers, slowly squeezing the city until you could hardly breathe. A low growl of thunder echoed up the cavern of Fifth Avenue and I looked up to where the sky started at the seventy-first floor of the Empire State Building. I could smell the rain. It was the kind that hung above the orderly piles of concrete until it was soaked with dust and debris and when it came down it wasn't rain at all, but the sweat of the city."

Spillane often starts with action, but here ... as with McBain and Chandler, it's about mood and establishing the first-person voice. Leonard doesn't give two shits about ambiance, and that's fine—he's up to something else. But calling what he does to open a novel a "rule" is nonsense.

How about "avoid prologues"?

MAC: There is nothing wrong with a prologue, if it serves a purpose. Something in the past that has a shape and meaning that will impact the rest of the story can be useful and create reverberations throughout the narrative. Why tell writers they should avoid something? Why limit their toolbox? Leonard is a carpenter telling his apprentices to use a hammer and nails, but for God's sake don't touch a screwdriver and screws. Ask me about this some more. This is fun.

Leonard's next rule was to never use a verb other than "said" to carry dialogue. What are your thoughts on that?

MAC: I almost agree with that. Avoidance of "said" in pursuit of not repeating a word calls attention to itself in an embarrassing, amateur way. It's the "never" that bothers me. Sometimes "blurted" or "shouted" or their brethren work well and mix things up just enough while lending emphasis. Deadpan understatement is not the only way. Hammett didn't write like Chandler, and Chandler didn't write like Hammett, despite their linkage.

How about "never use an adverb to modify the verb 'said,' such as 'he admonished gravely'"? Leonard called this a mortal sin. Do you believe this, and do you feel there are mortal sins when it comes to writing?

MAC: Again, it's the "never"—writers love to teach beginning writers that adverbs and adjectives are evil. Stephen King has said this, and of course his books are littered with both. Which is not a bad thing— why deny yourself perfectly useful tools? I agree that any time a verb can carry its own weight, that's a good thing. But why limit yourself? As for "sins," it's a sin to pretend the strategies and style you've developed through hard work and brains is exactly how all other fiction writers should operate.

His next rule was not go crazy with exclamation points, which I agree with. Those always stand out to me. He said a writer shouldn't use more than three per 100,000 words, which seems very specific. He did, however, say Tom Wolfe was the exception. What are your thoughts on this?

MAC: I agree with that, to a degree. The notion that you can use "three per 100,000 words" is probably just Leonard being cute—he surely knew there was no recipe to writing (note the "surely" as a qualifier, which is different from just plain "knew"). But like a lot of these rules, they apply to third-person narrative, not first, where the excitability of a narrator might lead to seeming over-use of exclamation points, in pursuit of characterization. Mike Hammer uses quite a few exclamation points, excitable boy that he is.

Another rule was to never use the words "suddenly" or "all hell broke loose."

MAC: This one I also almost agree with, and "all hell broke loose" is a cliché, of course. "Suddenly" might be used once in a while.

Rule number seven was to use regional dialect sparingly.

MAC: Finally a good rule, but a flawed one. I would argue that *The Adventures of Huckleberry Finn* (1884) is a pretty good book. One of my favorite writers is Mark Harris and his Henry Wiggen novels, which employ a barely literate first-person narrator. It matters whether your narrator is Nabokov's Humbert Humbert or Cain's Frank Chambers. A lot of these later Leonard rules don't allow for first-person narrators to sound like real people and not professional writers. Such a narrator might employ clichés, for example. Oh, and isn't Leonard using a modifier there, by way of "sparingly"? Wasn't there a verb available that could carry the load alone?

Leonard's next rule was to avoid using detailed descriptions of characters. He uses Ernest Hemingway's "Hills Like White Elephants" (1927) as an example of what can be achieved without description. In that story the closest Hemingway comes to character description is, "She had taken off her hat and put it on the table." What do you think about this one?

MAC: From my point of view, omitting descriptions of characters is sheer laziness. I don't necessarily mean laziness on Leonard's part, although much of what he advises novelists comes from his screenwriting training. Screenwriters are encouraged to leave character description fairly blank to allow variant casting choices, and screenplays are often stripped down generally so as not to step on the jobs of art direction, costuming, and so on. I go back to strategy—Leonard's strategy is to leave this work to the reader. Mine is to share with the reader what I see. Fiction is a collaboration between writer and reader, and I like to maintain control in that collaboration. Take Hammett, who is a damn spare writer in many ways—but he opens *The Maltese Falcon* (1930) with his detailed "blond Satan" description of Sam Spade. On the other hand, Spillane never describes Mike Hammer as a strategy to encourage identification with the reader, who becomes "I." Strategies, not rules.

Leonard next advises us not to go into great description about places and things as he believed such descriptions bring the story to a standstill.

MAC: I understand the impulse not to slow down the story, but descriptions of places and things create both sense of place and characterization. You describe the apartment where a character lives, and you know who that person is. This is a valuable tool that a fiction writer can use to varying degrees. I am at times criticized for describing setting and, for example, going into detail about what a character is wearing. I may well overdo it. But, again, I want to control the reader's experience, and, anyway, what a character is wearing is characterization. The opening of *The Big Sleep* (1939), in which the Sternwood mansion is described, is vital to the book, and the description of the General in the hothouse of orchids is key.

The last of Leonard's rules is his most famous: "Try to leave out the parts readers skip," which are long, dense paragraphs of prose.

MAC: Well, I might suggest, in the first place, writing those parts in an interesting way—Chandler again, in that opening of *The Big Sleep*, is giving you vivid stuff you want to read. I would also suggest not writing to the lowest common denominator—I am not in the business of looking out for the interests of readers with ADD. A lot of readers do skip parts, but not always the same parts. For example, when I read about a film director or novelist, and plot summaries of their works are presented, I skip them, even while understanding those passages were proper to include. And other readers skim instead of skip. Readers read some parts of a novel at 25 miles per hour, others at 100. Here I really do suspect Leonard of being lazy. I will say this—these days I avoid long paragraphs, even breaking up descriptive passages. James M. Cain said that the eye loves a ragged right margin, and he was right.

Then again, I remember a story Don Westlake told me. He and John

D. MacDonald were on a cruise, one of those things where fans mingle with creators. Every morning, a short story written by the celebrity mystery writers was circulated among the attendees for discussion later. MacDonald and Westlake were not well-acquainted, but knew of each other of course, and one morning on deck MacDonald approached Westlake and said, "I'm not sure the way you set things up in your story was fair to the reader." Westlake said, "Fuck the reader." MacDonald grinned and shook Westlake's hand, and a friendship was formed.

You mentioned reading both Leonard and George V. Higgins early on. Both were masters of dialogue, but whose dialogue did you prefer? While on the surface they look similar, they're actually quite different. I love Higgins, but his saying "Jackie said" or whatever character "said" after almost every line in The Friends of Eddie Coyle *(1970) distracts me a bit. My thought always was, if there are only two characters involved in the conversation, then the reader knows who's saying what if the writer only sprinkles in the occasional "said." What are your thoughts on the two writers' styles?*

MAC: I haven't read Higgins since the day in 1971 or '72 when I realized I was unconsciously imitating him. Leonard is a great writer of dialogue—as with Cain, dialogue is the engine. And I was reading Leonard long before I was reading Higgins. I'm talking about things like *The Moonshine War* (1969) and *Hombre.*

I consider dialogue one of my strengths, but I am still working on it, listening to people talk by way of research. In my paperback original days, I didn't use much stage management. I was encouraged, back in the seventies, to start adding stage management because that style of dialogue writing was thought of as being endemic to pulp writing, paperback original writing, and my agent was taking me into the hardcover market. So rather reluctantly I started putting in stage business.

Now I've come to like it, and see such interruptions as sources of characterization and rhythm. I've also started identifying the speaker before the first line of dialogue. Fiction writing is always a work in progress, or should be. There's a rule for you.

You found yourself imitating Higgins' dialogue, so you decided to stop reading him. But you never had that problem with Leonard. Why do you think that is? What was different for you?

MAC: That's easy. I was reading Leonard before I became a professional. I can read people like Larry Block, Don Westlake, Mickey [Spillane], Ed McBain, because I encountered them as a fan. Leonard was in that group. I sold my first book in 1971. People like [Rex] Stout and [Agatha] Christie and even James M. Cain were still active. Writers like that, and of course Spillane and McBain and John D. and Ross McDonald, they weren't the competition. They were all to be read and admired and learned from. People who started around when I did, and everyone who came after, that's the competition.

Leonard always said he wanted to make himself invisible in his writing and make people forget there's a writer, but I think an argument can be made that his exceedingly slick, stylized writing, which I love, actually made his presence more noticeable. I think his voice ends up being stronger than his characters. It's a thoroughly enjoyable and easy-to-listen-to voice, but it's very distinctive and strong. Your Hard Case Crime colleague Jason Starr told me he believed that where "series" readers who read things like Jack Reacher or Easy Rawlins novels come back again and again to see those characters, Leonard readers return for Leonard, who essentially becomes his own character. What are your thoughts on that?

MAC: Those are smart observations—both yours and Jason Starr's. Westlake told me that good writing is invisible, and I sort of agree with that. Film editing is the same—flashy editing takes you out of the narrative. I dislike fiction writing that would rather impress than entertain. But now and then, you do something a little bit showy—throw a prize in among the Cracker Jacks. Leonard was all style and that does bring his presence to the writing, as do the choices he makes. I try to make Nate Heller and Quarry good company—people we like spending time with in the pages of a book, even if we'd recoil at really spending time with such people, Quarry particularly. I love Rex Stout, but his mysteries—which seem compelling while you're reading them—just disappear while Archie and Wolfe are eternal.

A final word about Leonard's rules—they are useful to understand his approach. As rules for other writers, they only serve to teach you how to write like Elmore Leonard, which is pointless, because we already have a perfectly good one of those.

Similar to Stephen King, there have been a few very good film adaptations of Leonard's work and a lot of bad ones. As a writer who has not only had his own work adapted to screen to varying degrees and who has also written and directed films himself, why do you feel that so many Leonard adaptations fail to capture the essence of his work? This has always struck me as being strange considering the books themselves feel so cinematic.

MAC: That's a tough one to answer. There have been some really good ones, actually—the original *3:10 to Yuma* (1957), *The Tall T* (1957), *Hombre* (1967), *Jackie Brown* (1997), *Get Shorty* (1995), *Valdez Is Coming* (1971) ... *52 Pick-Up* (1986) is pretty good, and I have a soft spot for *Moonshine War* (1970) and *Mr. Majestyk* (1974). Actually that's a pretty good track record for film adaptations, most of which get him. And I would kill for a TV series as good as *Justified* (2010). As I look at the list, though, I think it's his earlier work that translates best—he was still plotting, not just riffing.

5

S.A. Cosby

S.A. Cosby toiled at a number of jobs, including bouncer, forklift operator, and construction worker, before finding success as a writer. He published his first novel, *Brotherhood of the Blade: The Invitation*, in 2015. He then made a name for himself with his short fiction appearing in anthologies such as *Fast Women and Neon Lights: Eighties Inspired Neon-Noir* (2016) and *Thuglit: Last Writes* (2016). His story "Slant-Six" received an honorable mention in *Best American Mystery Stories of 2016*.

In 2019, Cosby published his impressive sophomore novel, *My Darkest Prayer*. That same year, he was awarded an Anthony for Best Short Story for "The Grass Beneath My Feet."

However, it was his third novel, *Blacktop Wasteland* (2020), that established him as a literary powerhouse. The crime novel received near-unanimous rave reviews and praise from novelists as varied as Dennis Lehane, Lee Child, R.L. Stine, and Walter Mosley. (Mosley credited it with single-handedly reinventing the American crime novel.) It also appeared on just about every "best of" 2020 literary list in existence.

Cosby considers himself a student of Elmore Leonard (among other writers). As such, *Blacktop Wasteland* has been widely compared to Leonard's work (although Cosby's style is uniquely his own). In a starred review, *Library Journal* wrote that the novel took place "in Elmore Leonard land...." *BookPage* called it a combination of *Bullitt* (1968), *The Fast and the Furious* (2001), and "gritty Elmore Leonard–style noir."

At the time of this writing, Cosby's *Blacktop* follow-up, *Razorblade Tears*, was nearing release.

ANDREW J. RAUSCH: *Do you remember your first encounter with Elmore Leonard's work?*

S.A. COSBY: I'll give you a little backstory. I grew up in a very small Southern town, and I grew up really poor. Once a week we would go up to the local thrift store and find clothes and socks for us. We couldn't afford to go to the regular stores like Woolworths. In this thrift store was a bin, like a shopping cart, full of paperbacks. For a dollar, you could buy five paperbacks. I would always pull random books out of there. I didn't really read the back. I was 12 or 13. I just liked reading, so I'd go grab a handful of books. One of the books I pulled out one time was *Swag* (1976), which is also known as *Ryan's Rules*. I went home and I read that book. It wasn't the first book that made me want to be a writer. It wasn't the first book that made me think I could do it. But it was the first book that made me realize that writing—specifically crime writing—can be an art form. It's not just a pulpy way you can spend an afternoon. You can create characters that leap off the page. And create characters that have real situations, but still make it fun and exciting.

I was about twelve or thirteen when I read *Ryan's Rules,* and when I finished it, I was like, "Wow, this guy.... I don't know what he's doing different from Mickey Spillane or Mike Shayne or people like that, but man, this is something different." From then on, I devoured anything by him that I could get my hands on.

Swag is a terrific novel. It's my favorite of Leonard's.

SAC: *Swag* is a great novel, especially in building tension by escalation. At first, they knock over a couple liquor stores. They knock over this, they knock over that. Ryan's got his rules that they're supposed to follow. And over the course of the book, they break every rule and end up paying the price. It's great foreshadowing and world building. And world building in the way that it's a real world taking place in Detroit in the '70s.

The dynamic between Stick and Frank is marvelous. Frank begins the book thinking Frank's going to be a little smarter than Stick and that Stick is just going to be his muscle. But by the middle of the book, Frank realizes, no, Stick is my equal; maybe even a little bit smarter than I am.

The ending is great too because it's one of those... Oh man, they almost got away with it, but she left the fucking note! *Ohhhhh!* It's one of those books! It's funny because I read an interview with him where he said he never intended to write about Stick again, and he just kind of hung around in his head, so he wrote another! I took a lot of inspiration from Stick for characters that I've written about. Characters who are more deep and more complex than they may appear.

It's interesting that characters like Stick and some of his others come and go in different stories.

SAC: Leonard does the thing other people were doing, but it's interesting to look at now with the breadth of his career. He created a shared universe where characters pop up in other books. People are referenced. It gives all of his works—especially his Detroit novels—connectivity that really just makes you feel immersed in his world. Of course, he moved on to doing things in the '20s era with *The Hot Kid* (2005) and stuff like that, but those Detroit novels.... They're very similar to the movies at that time. The '70s and '80s, when you had these really gritty, blue collar crime novels and movies. It feels like a lived-in world.

Leonard writing about a location he really knows inside out comes through in those Detroit novels. I think maybe those novels are grittier partially because of the locale.

SAC: Definitely. He knew those streets. He knew those alleyways. He knew those abandoned lots, those shuttered factories. You could feel it. You could almost smell it coming off the page. I love it. The Florida novels are more, and this isn't a word ... hijinx-y.

And they're more polished.

SAC: A little more polished. If you read *Riding the Rap* (1995) or *Pronto* (1993) or *Maximum Bob* (1991), those novels, are fun and they're fast paced and excellent, but they do seem a little bit lighter in tone. Those Detroit novels, especially *52 Pickup* (1986), are dark books. That book in particular is a dark, gritty book. By the time you finish reading it, you're like, "I gotta take a bath!" But in a good way.

It's also, in my opinion, one of the first adaptations of a film that got the feel of the book. Roy Scheider is great. Clarence Williams III. John Glover. A really great adaptation of the novel. Those characters are very similar to the ones in the book. Like I said, it's a very dark novel. Don't get me wrong, a lot of people get killed in the Florida novels, but those just seem a little bit lighter; not quite as heavy. And also, more of a hero/villain dynamic, especially in the *Raylan* novels [*Pronto, Riding the Rap, Fire in the Hole*, 2001, *Raylan*, 2011]. Raylan is obviously the hero and guys like the Zip are the villains. There's much more of a traditional Western literature style. Good guy/bad guy. With the Detroit novels, it's very much a state of grace. It's very much a situation where, yeah, we're pulling for these dudes or gals, but man, they're bad people. They're not people I want to have dinner with.

A lot more antiheroes in those.

SAC: Definitely. That's one of those things that Leonard was able to do well. The only other person that comes to mind who did it as well was

Donald Westlake when he was writing those Richard Stark novels. In the Parker novels, he creates these workaday blue-collar antiheroes who aren't nice people, but it's almost like you respect their skill. You respect them so much that you want them to get away with it.

Killshot (1989) is one of my favorites. It's in the top fifteen. *Killshot* is a pretty simple story. Hitman gets seen by a witness. The guy eliminates the witness. But the way he writes the relationship between Blackbird and Richie. When Blackbird kills Richie.... I'm pretty swift with books. I'm pretty sure I know when things are happening, but I did *not* see that coming. When you go back and read it again, you see it coming because he just does not respect Richie as a person. Richie is not professional. He's a fool. He's stupid. He makes dumb mistakes. By the time he shoots him through that bubble of chewing gum, which is great imagery, he's had enough. He's had it. He sees himself as a professional. The whole world sees him as a brutal killer, but he sees himself as a professional. He has a certain code, and Richie just shits all over that code. Again, tension by escalation. One thing happens and then another. This domino falls, another domino falls.

The plot is great. But for my money, there is nobody better with dialogue. *Ever.* I mean that, and not in just crime novels, but in general. Nobody catches the rhythm of the way people really talk better than Elmore Leonard. I think Dennis Lehane comes close, but with Elmore Leonard you feel like you're eavesdropping on a conversation when you're reading his books.

Dialogue has always been something I've focused on in my own writing. I've studied the other masters like David Mamet, Shane Black, and Quentin Tarantino, but even those guys don't come close to Leonard. His dialogue sounds amazingly authentic, whereas some of their dialogue sounds too slick to be real.

SAC: He's incredibly organic. He wrote the rules a lot of writers don't like, but I think the secret is something he said in an interview. "Anything that sounds like writing, take it out." It's so simplistic, but it's hard to do. As a writer, you get enamored with your soliloquies and your lines—your punch lines, so to speak. You always kind of want to end the chapter on a good line. I think as a writer you have to work to get away from that if you want your book to maintain a sense of realism. I find myself doing that. I've got to pull back. I've got to pull back on the metaphors. I've got to pull back on the soliloquies. Write the way people actually talk to each other. The way people actually have conversations. The lulls, the pauses, the stammering, the way people cut each other off.

I think, like you said, Mamet is really good at that. Tarantino's one of the best at it in film. But in writing, it's difficult for writers to get that right because we fall in love with language to such an extent that sometimes we find ourselves writing long, verbose, flowery sentences and those darlings that we don't want to kill. I never got to meet Mr. Leonard personally, but he seemed ruthless. He didn't mind cutting his darlings at all. You see it in his writing. You see it in his stories.

And his plots! They aren't overly complicated. You could summarize most of his plots in two or three sentences. I think that is also one of his strengths.

I think that's true, but it's also deceptive. They seem very simplistic until you really analyze them, like Rum Punch *(1992).*

SAC: I agree. On the surface, it's deceptively simple. Like *Pagan Babies* (2000). Here's these three characters trying to get this money [and] they're using this charity as a front. But when you read the book, oh my god! The IRA is involved. There's these Cuban nationals. There's this former cop who's a heavy now. There's this lady who used to be a nun but she drinks. Like I said again, you can describe the plots in a couple sentences. Three grifters try to steal money and use a charity as a front. But when you get to the end, it's like a Russian doll. Once you get into the book, it's like, "What is this?"

The most recent book I read of his was *Road Dogs* (2009). Another deceptively simple book. Jack Foley's out of prison and wants to retire to Florida and chill. Doesn't want any problems. But he gets caught in this crazy, crazy situation with this fake medium and gangsters and drug dealers. And again, a Russian doll of a plot that just unfolds. By the end of the book, you're like, "What the fuck just happened?" I think sometimes he had deceptively simple plots with complex endings.

His books were always lean and mean, but Road Dogs *was the one that really shows how much you can do almost exclusively through dialogue. It has very little exposition.*

SAC: I admire Elmore Leonard. He's on my Mount Rushmore of great writers. Another thing is that I used to have a problem with descriptions of layouts of buildings. That was my weak point. I don't know why. There were times when I'd write about a building or a structure or something, and it would have to be 480 feet long. It didn't make any sense. And he had a way of just, in a couple sentences ... you go in, there's an ottoman, there's a kitchen to your right, something to your left. I stole that! I had to get away from that. Unless you're writing a Tom Clancy spy novel, the layout of the house or the mobile home or wherever the action takes place isn't super important. It's a set piece. Here's your guys or your gals and this is where they're talking. Or this is where they're fighting or where a gun fight is going to break out. Again, just the minimalist approach he took to writing, again, is deceptive. Because it looks deceptive, but like you said, he's packing so much in that dialogue. And he's doing that with internal monologues, too. Whatever the character is saying to the person that he or she is talking to is one thing, and then we've got this other monologue going on inside that's like, you just lied to that person. Or they're lying to you.

And then to do all that and still have surprises.... Again, it's something you either have or you don't. You're either born with it or you ain't. He had it in spades, I think. Even when he stepped out of his comfort zone. He's so versatile. He did a lot of Westerns, and even those Westerns still maintain that sense of minimalism. That sense of dialogue-driven action. Or the ones I call his prohibition novels, like *The Moonshine War* (1969) or *The Hot Kid*. Different circumstance, different time period, but it still feels fresh and raw and propulsive. Again, it goes back to his mastery of dialogue.

As a black writer, what do you think about the way he writes black characters?

SAC: I think the way he writes characters of color should be a masterclass for anybody that is not a member of an ethnicity. What he does, for instance, let's use Ordell in *Rum Punch*. The way Ordell talks is not caricature; it's character. He's a character who happens to be black. I don't want to speak for Mr. Leonard. He's deceased now, but I don't think he ever went into writing a black character or a Hispanic character with the idea of "I'm going to write the definitive black character." I think he wrote his characters like, "Wouldn't it be interesting with this character, who happens to be black, to decide to hook up with this character he was in prison with and try to sell guns?" Or in *Pagan Babies*, "Wouldn't it be cool if this guy who's very quiet and very thoughtful, who happens to be a Cuban refugee, is the guy who ends up with the money?"

I think a lot of writers, and I'll use famous writers or screenwriters, have a certain fetishization of black characters. For instance, some of the characters in Quentin Tarantino's works. By no means, I am not disparaging Quentin, and I think he's a great director, but I do think there's a certain amount of fetishization. There's a certain amount of, "Hey look, I created this cool black character and I want you guys to really rally around me because I did this."

I never got that with Elmore Leonard. Whether it's Ordell in *Rum Punch*, or Sportree in *Swag*, or any of his black or Hispanic characters. It never comes off as tone deaf or fetishization. It never felt shoehorned. I think it's because he wrote the characters first and added ethnicity later. What I mean is, he came up with a character and knew what he wanted the character to do within the confines of the story, and then he was like, "Okay, this character is gonna be Hispanic." I bet you if you were to ask him if he was still around, that he probably did talk to people who were Hispanic. He did research. He found out certain things that are germane to Hispanic culture. Some things are germane to black culture. I think he did his due diligence. I think a lot of people get their panties in a bunch with sensitivity readers. "I don't want a sensitivity reader." Okay, then just call it research. I think Elmore Leonard did his research.

I think one of the great things he did that a lot of writers don't do is he *evolved* as he wrote. His black characters in the '70s sound like black characters in the '70s. His Hispanic characters he wrote in the '90s sound like Hispanic characters of the '90s. It goes back to being a great listener. I think that's something he did. Not all his books are perfect, but I think he *seemed* to—I never met the man personally—but he seemed to put a really great effort into trying to make the characters real and not just caricatures. I think that's something a lot of folks could learn from.

Do you have any favorite Elmore Leonard characters?

SAC: Yeah. If I had to give my top three.... Stick. I love Stick. I think I like Stick because I'm a Southern boy and Stick was a transplanted Southerner that ended up in Detroit. People always underestimated Stick in the books because he had a Southern drawl. They heard that Southern drawl and they're like, "He's just a dumb redneck, a big dumb redneck." And nine times out of ten he's the smartest person in the book.

A lot of people don't talk about *Killshot*, but I was very moved by the character Armand Degas. I'm going to sound very pretentious, but I'm going to say it anyway: *Killshot* is almost *Death of a Salesman* for hitmen. Because Armand starts the book, he's got a job he's doing and he's gotta kill this old mafia guy. They have a very pleasant conversation right before he kills him. And you get the feeling that Armand's doing it and it's his job, but he sees that his way of life is passing by. All through the book, he contemplates his own mortality. He contemplates death. Yeah, he's trying to kill this witness. Yeah, he doesn't want to go to jail. But he's a very moving character for me.

My third favorite Elmore Leonard character is Harry Arno. He's crazy, he's tough, he's wild, he's like a real person. Because he's not a great hero. Because he takes credit for saving Raylan's life when he really didn't. He's just this weird little nerdy dude that I wouldn't mind having a drink with. I could see myself walking into a bar and having a drink with Harry Arno.

Those are the three that stand out for me personally. I like all those characters. I think Ordell from *Rum Punch* is an interesting character. I think Louis Gara from *Rum Punch* is a great character. His characters are real and lived-in people that are sometimes dumb. Smart people who make bad decisions. Like *Mr. Majestyk* (1974). A lot of people who think of *Mr. Majestyk*, they're thinking of the movie. Charles Bronson, quiet, violent, contemplative. If you read the book, Mr. Majestyk is suffering from what we would call today PTSD. The violence that is forced upon him in that book is a real struggle for him. If you read the book, he tries for a long time not to respond. He's trying. He's a quiet man, so to speak. That's a real, lived-in character. I think *Mr. Majestyk* has a little bit of that early '70s alpha-male bluster. There are a couple lines in there now that are a little dated, but as a whole he's a great character who's very deep and complex.

I think Leonard, maybe more than any other crime writer, was way more invested in the characters and their depth and complexity. His characters aren't just props. I love English mysteries, which sounds crazy with the stuff I write. I love Agatha Christie. But a lot of times when you read those books, the characters are just props. They're chess pieces to be moved around so you can get to this clever mystery and can figure out it's Professor Plum in the library with the wrench. With Elmore Leonard's stuff, the characters drive the story. The choices that his real-life, tough characters make is what drives the stories. They don't work in service to the story, the story works in service to them. It's a really interesting ability to have. I think when you look at some of the writers who came after him, you can see the influence. You can see it in Lehane and George Pelecanos. To a lesser extent, I wouldn't say Walter Mosley in so much as in the type of writing, but in those lived-in characters. Those real-life problems that these characters have. That's the thing that always drew me to Elmore Leonard. Yes, Stick's an armed robber, but he's got to make rent. Blackbird, he's a hitman, but he's also got arthritis and he's getting older. A friend of mine calls it the Spiderman motif. Spiderman's a superhero, but he can't cash a check because it was written out to Spiderman. Leonard really excels at that. There's a whole generation of writers that came behind him—some better than others—that were influenced by him. Sometimes we all dip into that well, and I look for it in my writing to make sure I'm not doing it too much to the point that it becomes pastiche.

I think he looms large over crime writing in the 20th century. He really does.

Do you see Elmore Leonard being an author who will still be read in 50 or 100 years?

SAC: Yeah. If you want to put him on that Mount Rushmore of great American crime writers or just great American writers. I think it's [Raymond] Chandler. It's Leonard. I think, it's to a lesser extent, Mosley. And I think it's great writers like that that'll be read. It'll never go out of print. I think there's a lot of great writers from the '50s and '60s, or '40s and '50s, that people don't really read anymore. People don't really read Ross MacDonald like they used to. People don't really read John D. Mac-Donald like they used to. There was a time when Mickey Spillane was one of the number one writers in the world.

It's not to say that their writing is of less quality, but there's something timeless about the work of Elmore Leonard. I think you could pick up *City Primeval* (1980) right now and read it. Just sit down for an afternoon, and you will not only have a really great story, but again, you have these incredibly complex and interesting characters. He's up there with those guys and those gals. I think he'll be up there with Patricia Highsmith. I think he's a name that people will always want to go back to, because at the end of the day he wrote about real people who got into crime.

The thing that I love about him that influenced my writing, personally, is that you got a real sense of why these people were doing what they were doing. Why they made this choice. I think that's what separates great crime writing from good crime writing. It's the idea of "this person is not just a bank robber" or "this person is not just a criminal" or "this person is not just a gunrunner." There's a reason why this person's like this. There's a reason this person's making this decision. I think he did it with such a fine touch. It's not ever heavy-handed. It's never, "Message! Look, here's a message!" But you do get messages. I'll go back to *Pagan*

Babies. There's a character that's a Cuban refugee that the main character is working with to get this money. He's a quiet character. You get some of his internal monologue, and he doesn't talk a lot, but by the end of that book, you realize that this is the guy that came over the Cuban boat lift that's suffering. He's seen horrible, horrible things. By the end of the book, I was rooting for him because of what he had been through!

I'll tell you another character like that: Bobby Shy in *52 Pickup*. He's a brutal killer. He's a guy not to be trifled with, but he's also a guy who's in Detroit in the '70s when the Ford motor plant was moving out. Here's a guy that looks like he has no other options. Of course, people who lived that life will say "Oh, he's always got an option," but when you read that book and the little touches here and there that Bobby says, you realize, no. Yeah, he could've gone a different way, but we understand why he went this way.

I think that's what's going to endure with Elmore Leonard. And they're just great fucking stories. They're never boring. They're never trite. They're always interesting. Some of them are funny as hell. Some of them are interesting and suspenseful as hell. And I think he did the things that Raymond Chandler did. I know it doesn't seem like there's a lot of comparison between the two guys, but he made the simple look complex and the complex look really simple. And trust me, it's not! [Laughs.] As a writer, I have tried to write in that style of both of these gentlemen I respect a great deal. It is not simple. And that's where the genius lies.

6

David Geherin

David Geherin served as professor of English Language and Literature at Eastern Michigan University from 1969 through to his retirement in 2010. There he taught such courses as "Mystery and Detective Fiction" and "Murder in Literature." Recognized as an expert on crime fiction, Geherin has written many books on the subject, including *Sons of Sam Spade: The Private-Eye Novel in the 70s* (1980), *The American Private Eye: The Image in Fiction* (1985), and *Scene of the Crime: The Importance of Place in Crime and Mystery Fiction* (2008).

He has written several books studying the works of individual authors in *John D. MacDonald* (1982), *Elmore Leonard* (1989), and *Carl Hiaasen: Sunshine State Satirist* (2018). His book on Leonard was the first significant full-length study of the author and his work. Geherin has since contributed to *Critical Essays on Elmore Leonard* (2020), edited by Charles Rzepka.

ANDREW J. RAUSCH: *When did you first discover Elmore Leonard's work, and what do you remember about that experience?*

I began reading Leonard in the late seventies. At the time he was being regularly reviewed in the Detroit newspapers because he lived in the area and his novels were set in Detroit. As someone who also lived near Detroit, I was struck by how he used local settings so effectively.

What elements of Leonard's work would you say most resonate with you?

I love his humor and the way he introduces a new set of characters in virtually every novel. I recently wrote a book on Carl Hiaasen, who admits to being strongly influenced by Leonard. He followed Leonard's example of gathering together a new cast of colorful characters each time and allowing the story to grow out of their interactions.

Do you think his career trajectory would have been much different if he had written a series?

It would be different, and I don't think it would be quite as influential. In some ways, a series character is an easy way out for publishers and writers. But many writers get trapped by a series and kind of lose interest, yet they continue to churn out books. It's hard to maintain freshness in a long series. For Leonard, every book was a new start and that kept him interested as a writer. I think he could have been a successful writer of a series, but I don't think he would've established the reputation for originality that he did by doing it his way.

Leonard is frequently acknowledged by general readers as being one of the greatest crime writers ever, but his name, like other crime writers, has often been left out of literary conversations. Why do you think this is? Do you think this is simply a disrespect for the genre, or do you see there being other factors?

I think he has begun to get respect from the literary world. Martin Amis, for example, was a big fan and interviewed Leonard several times. Leonard was also awarded The National Book Foundation's Medal for Distinguished Contribution to American Letters in 2012, the first time it was given to a crime writer. He has a strong crossover appeal and I think he's broken out of the genre prison more than a lot of other crime writers have been able to.

Fair enough. Do you believe Leonard starting to be more acknowledged outside genre circles will continue to gain steam?

I think so. Charles Rzepka has just published a collection of scholarly essays on Leonard [*Critical Essays on Elmore Leonard*]. And his papers are now at the University of South Carolina, along with [F. Scott] Fitzgerald's. I think the literary establishment, to some degree, considers Leonard one of their own.

In your book, you talk about looking through Leonard's papers at the University of Detroit library. Have those things been relocated, or are some of his papers in both libraries?

I think they're still located in both places. I saw a lot of his early unpublished writings in the collection at the University of Detroit, his alma mater. I believe the material at the University of South Carolina is much more extensive.

What were your interactions with Leonard like?

Very, very enjoyable. I did four or five interview sessions with him at his home over a two-year period. He was generous with his time and with his materials. I remember the first time I went to interview him, he brought me down to his basement and began digging through his files to find old screenplays and unpublished stories he could lend me. He also had a wonderful sense of humor and didn't take himself that seriously. It wasn't, "Hey, I'm famous, my face is on the cover of *Newsweek* magazine." He was always kind of thrilled and surprised at the attention he was getting. Because success came late in life for him, he always put it in perspective.

I think it's telling that he didn't really pay attention to things like that. In your book, you mention his not knowing he'd been listed in Playgirl *magazine's list of the sexiest men.*

I think he got a kick out of some of those things! Like getting letters from prisoners. Sometimes he was surprised where his name popped up. Instead of feeding an ego that needed it, it just pleased him and sometimes entertained him.

Do you think any of those letters from the prisoners worked their way into his writing?

That's a good question, and I don't have an answer to it. I assume prisoners might have appreciated his books because so many of his characters were similar to people they knew.

Leonard didn't find major acclaim until after he'd been writing for more than thirty years. In your book, you suggest his not being in the spotlight all that time possibly benefited his writing.

I think that the worst thing that can happen to many writers is have a big first novel, because then the pressure is on. How are you going to live up to that acclaim in your second book? There are so many examples of writers that never blossomed. I think it's great to have an apprenticeship that goes on for years and years. Leonard was certainly making a living, but he wasn't getting the acclaim. He could try new things. He wasn't responding to what people expected. I think that was great for him.

On the surface, a lot of his themes were the same. I think it would be easy for some to dismiss his work as the same. But over the years, there was a lot of experimentation in his evolution. You would see tweaks to his handling of character perspectives and other elements here and there.

As far as his characters go, he got to the point where he knew what he could do. He knew the kind of character that could talk. Why mess with that if you can continue to do it? Another thing that kept his books fresh was that he didn't limit himself to a single location. Certainly, he could have continued to grind out novels set in Detroit, using that city's gritty, blue-collar atmosphere, but he didn't. He moved his scene to Florida and wrote a couple of Florida novels that were very successful. And he could've continued to do that, but then he went to Atlantic City for *Glitz* (1985). And then he went to Hollywood for *Get Shorty* (1990). He ended up writing other books set in Italy, Dubai, Mississippi, New Orleans. He always found ways to find new characters and new places that would keep himself interested and it shows in his work.

Why do you think it took Leonard so long to be recognized on the level he finally was?

Good question. Why does one writer become a best-seller and another have trouble getting published? It's sometimes pure luck. Some writers get discovered early and perhaps don't quite deserve it, and others never get discovered. Some get discovered late. I don't know. It's may be a matter of marketing? Or switching to a new publisher? I think what helped Leonard was that when people read him for the first time in *Glitz* or *LaBrava* (1983), they discovered there was already a long list of novels by this guy. It's a great thrill for a reader to discover a writer and say, "Wow, there's a dozen books I can read while waiting for the next one!" Part of it is just a matter of luck, but if you continue doing it well, the chances are pretty good that sooner or later you might become a best-selling writer. It doesn't always happen, and it doesn't always happen to deserving writers, but I think in the case of Leonard, he was very deserving of his breakthrough.

Do you feel that his success changed anything regarding the way he wrote?

I'm not sure. Obviously, the success of the TV series *Justified* inspired him to write another Raylan book. I think that once he established his way of doing writing, he wasn't necessarily going to be influenced by what other people said about it. Now I know that isn't entirely true. Early in his career a woman reviewer in the *Detroit Free Press* took him to task for his portrayal of female characters. And he thought, maybe she's right. so he made a deliberate effort to pay more attention to his female characters in his next novel. As his career continued, however, I think he became confident enough in his writing that he wasn't going to let success alter what had been working well for him.

You mentioned the Raylan *(2012) novel. It seems like at the end of his life, he was writing things that were sequels to his work that had been produced for film and television. Rather than the early books that would feature recurring characters, the sequels seemed more like sequels to the films than the actual novels themselves. Do you have any thoughts on that?*

I think you're right. I don't think he would have written *Be Cool* (1999) if it weren't for *Get Shorty* (the film, 1995) or *Raylan* if it weren't for *Justified*. He was always hoping for a good film version of one of his novels and was frustrated for many years by disappointing efforts. I think he liked the characters of Chili Palmer and Raylan enough to go back and write another book about them, but he was at least partly inspired by the success of the film and TV versions based on those characters.

Why do you think screenwriters and filmmakers generally find difficulty capturing the flavor of an Elmore Leonard novel?

One element has to do with his style of humor. One of the things that bothered him about the film version of *Stick* (novel 1983, film 1985) was that it seemed like Burt Reynolds and the other actors would say a line and then pause for the laugh. Leonard's characters are funny because they don't realize they're funny. They're not trying to be funny. What they say strikes us as funny, but it's just part of their character. Up until Scott Frank came along, I don't think anybody really got the importance of letting the humor speak for itself.

How many good books just don't ever make good films? Not because the book wasn't good, and not because the book couldn't be made into a great film. It just wasn't made by the right people. I think Quentin Tarantino and Scott Frank got what Leonard was doing in his books. Most of Leonard's novels have been turned into films, but only a few of them were very good.

The writings of Ernest Hemingway and George V. Higgins influenced Leonard's work, but he came away with his own unique style. As a person who is knowledgeable of these writers, how would you compare and contrast his work to theirs'?

Hemingway was an influence on his writing from the very beginning. What he learned from him was simplicity of language. Nothing fancy. No adverbs. No metaphors. No lush descriptions. He differs from Hemingway in that he had a sense of humor that is missing in Hemingway's work. Higgins came at a time when he was making the transition from Westerns to crime stories and he learned from him what a crime

Perspectives on Elmore Leonard

novel could be by just letting the characters talk. Leonard once wrote a brief essay titled "What Elmore Leonard Does" (*Who's Writing This?* ed., Daniel Halpern 1994) where he gives his characters a chance to describe his method of writing: All they do is grumble and complain that "This guy makes us do all the work!"

What, in your mind, makes Elmore Leonard different from other crime writers that had preceded him and those who were his contemporaries?

He started writing his crime novels at a time when the hard-boiled private-detective novel was dominant, but he chose to go in a different direction. His characters were sometimes cops, but more often than not they were the bad guys.

Then there is his sense of humor. There is humor in many private-eye novels but most of it comes from the voice of the main character who is the narrator. Leonard's humor comes from the voices of a variety of different characters and in each one's own colorful language. I think that set him apart as well.

What novel or novels would you consider to be Leonard's masterpiece or masterpieces?

That's a tough question. I recently re-read all of Leonard's novels for an essay I was writing ["The Sense of Place in Elmore Leonard's Crime Fiction" in *Critical Essays on Elmore Leonard*, ed. by Charles Rzepka] and really liked several of the books from the 1980s, especially *Split Images* (1981), *Glitz* (1985) and *Freaky Deaky* (1988). All his novels are entertaining, but those stand out in my mind as being exceedingly well done.

Even though Leonard is most associated with the crime genre, he wrote a lot of things that were outside the genre. It's the general consensus that his crime work resonated best. What do you think it is about his crime work that stands above his other works?

I think it's the characters. The characters in those other books don't have the same kind of flavor they do in his crime novels. His reputation isn't harmed by them, but I don't think they add to it. A lot of successful writers of crime fiction have a desire to write standalone non-genre novels for any number of reasons. Leonard's *Touch* (1987) is a good example. It's a story he wanted to tell for a long time. But I generally don't find his non-genre novels as entertaining or as well done as his crime novels.

What ultimately made you decide to write your book about Leonard?

I had written a book (*The American Private Eye*, 1985) that was nominated for an Edgar Award. I was at the awards dinner with Bruce Cassiday, my editor, and we were at a table next to the one where Ed McBain, author of the popular 87th Precinct books, was seated. Bruce asked if I was interested in writing another book and suggested that McBain would make a good subject. I had read some of McBain's novels and I liked them a lot, but the more I thought about it, the more I began thinking about this local writer whose work I really liked and who didn't live far from where I did. Bruce agreed that Leonard would be a good choice, so I sent him a letter and told him I was planning to write a book about him. Shortly afterwards, he phoned and invited me to his home. And that's how the book began.

In the thirty years following the book's publication, have you have any reconsiderations or revelations regarding Leonard's work that you wish you could've included?

I'm happy with what I wrote, but I sometimes wish I had an opportunity to write about some of the novels he wrote after my book came out. I don't know that this would've changed what I had written. Since mine was the first book on Leonard, I saw it largely as an introduction to his work. I think that his later novels confirm many of the things I said about his writing in my book.

Everyone focuses on Leonard's strengths, but what do you objectively see as his weaknesses?

That's a good question. I don't always buy the male-female emotional relationships in many of his books. The film version of *Out of Sight* (1998) did a wonderful job portraying the relationship between George Clooney's character and Jennifer Lopez's. But I don't think he quite pulls that off in some of his other books. Certainly, his female characters became stronger as his career developed, but the relationships between the male and female characters I don't find necessarily work all that well.

Do you think people will be reading Elmore Leonard fifty years from now?

I think so. What makes Leonard such a popular author is that his books are flat-out entertaining. They're fun to read. I believe that their level of entertainment and the freshness of each novel will continue to draw readers to him. He is one of those crime writers whose books I believe will continue to be read for the same reason people still read Agatha Christie and Raymond Chandler. They hold up very well.

7

Cheryl Heuton
and Nicolas Falacci

Cheryl Heuton and Nicolas Falacci are a husband and wife television writing and production team. Falacci received his first screenwriting credit for the Karen Black-starring horror film *Children of the Night* (1991). The two of them later made a name for themselves as the co-creators and producers of the hit television series *Numb3rs*, which ran from 2005 to 2010. For their work on the series, the duo received the Carl Sagan Award for Public Understanding of Science in 2005. The series also received the National Science Board's Public Service Award in 2007.

Heuton and Falacci also co-wrote the pilot for a would-be USA Network television series titled *The Arrangement* which was based on Elmore Leonard's short story "When the Women Come Out to Dance" (2002). After USA opted not to move forward with the series, the pilot was then reedited into a feature-length film of the same title.

ANDREW J. RAUSCH: *Had either of you read Elmore Leonard's work prior to taking on this project?*
CHERYL HEUTON: I'd read it extensively.

What were your thoughts on his work? What were some of his novels that stood out to you?
CH: I loved *Freaky Deaky* (1988). I'm trying to think.... I mean, there are so many. And I've read books just because he *liked* them. I have *The Friends of Eddie Coyle* (1970) on my shelf and reread it every few years just because it was so important to him. There are so many of his books that I liked.... Lots of them.

How did you guys become involved with this project?
CH: Since we do pilots and do a lot of TV development, we were invited into a production company that had, at that time, been talking

to Elmore Leonard's granddaughter about a project he had given her the rights to. The company was The Mark Gordon Company. We've known Mark forever, but we were talking to someone who worked for Mark at the time, and they told us about a handful of projects. One of them was this short story that Elmore Leonard's granddaughter had the rights to called "When the Women Come Out to Dance" (2001), which is the titled story of a collection of short stories. They told us what it was about. That was the one that most interested us. They thought it could possibly be a TV show. I went and got the book, read the story, and thought I saw a great TV show there too. So we said, "Sure, we'd love to develop this." Then they called back and said, "There's a problem. The way we want to see the story, Elmore Leonard's granddaughter no longer sees it that way. But to be fair, she liked you guys, so we're going to bow out and you guys are free to talk to her."

We went directly to Elmore Leonard's granddaughter and sat down with her. She was working with a partner at the time, I don't remember her name. We sat down with them and told them how we saw the show. The granddaughter liked that. We said, "Let's see if we can set this up as a pilot right now." That began the process of working up a take on how the show would work and met with various production companies. There were a couple of them that wanted to do it, and a bunch of them that heard us and said "It's not for us." But the one that wanted to do it was the company that's a partnership between Doug Liman and David Bartis, which is called Hypnotic.

One of the reasons we went there was because one of our good friends was their TV development exec, Lindsay Sloane. Not the actress, the development exec. We had actually met with them in the past on other projects. We went in and told them the idea and they liked it. We decided to develop it as a pitch, which is a typical thing you do at this point. This was when streaming was very new, and cable was a real big outlet, but the first stop for most people on most projects was still the major networks. So we took it to the major networks and we had a pitch at NBC that went really well. They ended up making an offer on it, so we ended up not pitching it elsewhere. We developed it at NBC, where we got it to a point where we were really happy with it. And they were really happy with it. But the guy running NBC at the time didn't quite see it. His two number twos really liked it, and also it had been read by another guy.... Hypnotic had a tight relationship with USA [Network] because they're the producers of *Suits* and, at that time, *Covert Affairs*. They had let USA see the script and the guy who ran USA at the time,

Jeff Wachtel, really loved it. He kind of made it clear early on that if NBC didn't make it, USA wanted a shot at it. The head at NBC said, "If he's so crazy about it, let him make it."

So then we went over to USA, redeveloped it under Jeff, and we shot a pilot with them.

Nic mentioned you guys met with Elmore Leonard once?

CH: Yes, we did meet Elmore once. It was wonderful. We had lunch with him and his granddaughter, who controlled the rights to the story. It was her, her husband, Elmore Leonard, Elmore Leonard's long-time researcher [Greg Sutter], and the two of us at the Langham in Pasadena. He was out there during the television producer association event that happens once a year, and that year it was in Pasadena. He was out here because of *Justified*.

We had lunch. His researcher had read our pilot and really loved it. Elmore hadn't, so he wanted us to talk to him about it. It's kind of incredible. At this point he was still very sharp. This was not long before he died. *Very* sharp. Great insights with sense of story. Very interested. Short-term memory almost gone. So that's what we were dealing with. And his granddaughter told us about this and said, "Look, he may get argumentative, he may not like something he hears, but he'll forget it. And we can go on."

It wasn't quite that bad, but we had made changes. He always said he understood changes. *Justified* had made massive changes to his story. We had made changes, too. Some of the changes we made were changes that we wanted to make, but some of them were the changes that, to be frank, were ones USA wanted that we weren't that happy with. So we're talking him through some of that. "I love that." "Oh, that will work." "I see why you had to do that." And then at one point he said, "I don't see how that works. She never was a stripper." Then, "where's the dancing?" We were lucky enough to keep any housekeeping elements in it. USA was really trying to push it and make it into a story it really wasn't, which was a whole other thing. The works of Elmore Leonard were not a priority for that one guy at USA. It turned out to be a priority for a lot of other people there, and he miscalled that situation.

But Elmore was happy to hear about it. His researcher kept explaining TV to him, saying, "Well, they have to change the storyline to keep it continuing. They have to pull this other stuff in so that they can go back to it every week." Elmore did say at one point, "It was a short story in my head, so it starts and it's over. But I see what you're saying, that it's going to be a TV show like *Justified*. It can't be over." And yeah, that's why the bad guy survives the pilot in *Justified* but he's killed in the story.

Did he talk about any other television shows and what he believed worked or didn't work?

CH: I wouldn't say that he talked about why stuff worked and didn't work, but he did talk about things he liked and didn't like with *3:10 to Yuma* (2007), which amused him because it has two adaptations that were filmed fifty years apart or something. The amount of money he made for the first one [1957] was $5,000. When they remade it [in 2007], I think they paid him half of *that*. Because under that deal they had to pay him only fifty percent of what he'd gotten the first time, so it was $2,500. And he thought the ending of the new version was stupid. Which is interesting, because we're friends with the writers, and they totally agree with him. It was the director [James Mangold] of *3:10 to Yuma*'s decision to end it the way Elmore and the writers didn't like.

You mentioned that Jeff Wachtel didn't think see Elmore Leonard's name as being all that important. When you were pitching this around, did Leonard's name seem to have much cache in the TV world?

CH: It was huge. And this was even at a time when *Justified* was fairly new. I think any writer who's been a best seller is huge. A writer who's been a best seller whose work has been adapted to stuff like *3:10 to Yuma*—

NICOLAS FALACCI: *Get Shorty* (1995).

CH: Anyone with a profile like that is a big deal in TV. I have to say, it was big then, but now in 2019, it's way bigger. I was talking to some other writers and they were saying that some people won't even try with original stuff anymore.

What happened with The Arrangement? *Why did it die?*

CH: It died because USA was in a transition period where their shows that were considered—they used to call them blue sky, happy, fun, light, entertaining shows—weren't doing well anymore and they wanted to take a turn. That's why they originally did this. People there knew that Elmore Leonard was darker, edgier, would be more challenging. But Jeff Wachtel wasn't ready to embrace that. And he didn't quite understand. I mean, he knew intellectually that's what he had to do, but his gut, all his choices, on a day-to-day basis were towards lighter, funner [content]. He saw this as a chance to do a light romance set in Florida between a woman from Colombia and a white guy. And I was like, "That's how you see this?"

We pushed them. We pushed back the whole process the whole time. Plus, I think the casting was problematic. They turned down a lot of people who would've been great and cast a guy [Bryan Greenberg] who wasn't right for the part. That happens all the time—he just wasn't right for the part. The woman [Stephanie Sigman] was great. She's a regular now on *S.W.A.T.* Their other casting choices were great. Steven Root was a regular. Kumail Nanjiani was a regular. It was fantastic casting. Like a lot of networks, they had to learn the hard way. They fought us on Kumail Nanjiani, and then we cast him, and they wouldn't do a deal with him. They did a guest star role. The minute they got the first dailies, they were like, "This guy is astounding, we want to do a deal." We're like, "Too late." He was going on to do *Silicon Valley*.

The director [Kevin Bray] didn't really get the material, so we ended up with a lot of stuff that just had to be edited together to try to make it work. They kept trying to make it light and sunny. When Bonnie Hammer, the head of USA saw it, she was like, "Where's the Elmore Leonard? This is what we're supposed to be not doing, and you did it again?" And that was the end of that.

As you were continually getting all these story notes and new directions, how many different drafts of the pilot did you end up writing?

CH: I wouldn't be surprised if there were roughly ten major rewrites and thirty, forty different iterations.

NF: Polishes. We had to do a number of drafts for NBC, and then when we went to USA, obviously, they wanted a lot of changes.

CH: We're still very happy with what we did at NBC.

How did end up at HBO?

CH: It's not really at HBO. Well, I guess it is at HBO... HBO buys a lot of stuff they can program for odd and weird hours. It's also been sold overseas.

NF: My brother went to Mexico, and he's like, "I saw your pilot at the movies down in Mexico!"

CH: At the time, USA always asked you to do a longer version so that they would have the option of doing a mainstream TV movie. Which meant they had just enough material, more or less, and could cut it. But I don't know how well it holds together.

NF: Ninety minutes of that would be rough.

CH: Yeah, it would be rough.

Had you conceived any ideas of where the story might have gone in the future had it continued on?

CH: Yeah. Tons of ideas. You don't do a series without knowing what you want to do in the future. We wanted to do a woman who's from Colombia who's in Florida like a lot of Colombians, and who finds that a lot of her dark past has either followed her here or was here on its own accord. And she wants to make some personal reparations. She has a friend who's also Colombian that she kind of leans on to help her do some of this. Loosely based on, in Elmore's original story, it's a woman who knows these bad guys that come from her past. But when she goes into these households and finds out what's going on and where the wealth is, then they come and they all take it together. Our version of that was that she's using her past and her connections to not only get revenge and right some wrongs, but she's also going to go the other way. Everyone was interested in her righting these wrongs, like this Latin American version of *The Equalizer.*

We really wanted to feature *a lot* of characters from Mexico, Central America, and South America.

NF: Also, to sort of protect her survival in the United States, she had to make sure the man she married was successful.

CH: She basically marries a white politician who needs a Latino wife because he's trying to run for office in Florida. And he finds himself getting up against some really bad elements in Florida because that's how Florida operates. Very Elmore Leonard style. She has to start managing his career and protecting his clients.

NF: She also becomes this behind-the-scenes fixer for him.

How long did this entire process take, from your first shopping it around and for it then to be cut it into something full-length?

CH: We were involved about three years. How they took it and recut it into whatever kind of feature they have, we had no part of that.

Was it always titled The Arrangement?

CH: No. We just wanted to call it *When the Women Come Out to Dance* like it was in Elmore's original story. But USA didn't want to do that, so it was untitled. The entire time we were on it, it was "The Untitled Show." Then everyone was trying to come up with titles and no one could come up with anything good, and then they started trying to call it *The Arrangement*.

After you were forced to make all of these compromises, were there aspects of the final pilot that you were still pleased about?

CH: We're pleased about the casting of Stephanie Sigman. We must have auditioned over a hundred women. There were some really great actresses in there, but Stephanie, I still think, is going to be way bigger than just a supporting character on a CBS show. She was very good on *American Crime*. She's *really* good. I was thrilled to work with Stephen Root, a longtime favorite. We're still friends and thrilled that we got a chance to work with Kumail Nanjiani. We worked with a great DP, Jim Denault, and we worked with a great set designer [Barbara Peterson-Malesci]. Otherwise, a lot of frustrations, and that's TV pilots for you.

The pilot for *Numb3rs* was shot from top to bottom twice. The first time around, we had the wrong director and the wrong cast, just like this. But CBS gave us the chance to completely redo it, and we did. And then it ran six-and-a-half years.

NF: This time, we didn't get that chance.

Of all the Elmore Leonard adaptations you've seen, what do you think are some of the common denominators of the projects that do work and those that don't?

CH: Sticking to his tone, and also understanding that his tone is not a hundred percent dark. He has a comedic eye and a comedic ear. Understanding that and capturing that are important. You have to understand it's a very dark world, but it's comedic. Leonard has compassion. He doesn't just kill everybody.

NF: What we loved about his tone and the opportunity to try it ourselves—what really attracted us—is that he had very grounded characters and very grounded worlds, but his characters are colorful and funny. But they're not sitcom funny.

CH: Something we were able to express in our NBC version of our pilot is that the bad guys in Leonard's work aren't super-villains. They're not the smartest guys on the planet. They're often the dumbest guys in the story. And the scariest thing about them is how dumb they are.

8

Davey Holmes

Before working in television, Davey Holmes was a produced play-wright as well as a keyboardist for punk ska band the Mighty Mighty Bosstones. Holmes broke into television writing three episodes for the iconic series *Law & Order*, later serving as the series' story editor for two seasons. After that, Holmes wrote episodes for the series *3lbs.* and *Damage* before landing a recurring writing job on the series *In Treatment*. After having received a Writers Guild of America nomination in the category of New Series for *Damages* previously, Holmes won the same award in 2009 for *In Treatment*.

Holmes then wrote and served as a producer for a number of high-profile series (*Pushing Daisies*, *Happy Town*, *The Chicago Code*, and *Awake*). He next landed a gig as executive producer on the popular Showtime series *Shameless*. He also wrote seven episodes for the series and was nominated by the Online Film & Television Association for Best Writing in a Television Series for his work.

In 2017, Holmes served as series creator and showrunner on the Epix series *Get Shorty*, which took inspiration from the 1990 Elmore Leonard novel. Rather than crafting a direct adaptation, Holmes chose to re-imagine Leonard's storyline with different characters and simi-lar (but different) scenarios. Despite these dramatic changes, Holmes pulled off the impressive feat of maintaining the essence and feel of Leonard's writing.

ANDREW J. RAUSCH: *Had you read any of Leonard's work before you became involved with this project?*

DAVEY HOLMES: Absolutely. When I was twenty-five—I'm forty-nine now—I was already into his stuff and I remember hear-ing that they were making a movie of *Get Shorty*. I had a subscription to *Screenwriter* magazine, and the issue came with the script for *Get Shorty* in it. I had a Swiss-French girlfriend who wanted me to meet her parents. We were bumming around Europe. I remember I had this copy of the script in my backpack that I carried around Europe even though I had no affiliation whatsoever with that project, and no career (and wouldn't have a career for quite a while after that). But I was so taken with it that I was carrying it around.

Then I realized I wanted to read more than just *Get Shorty*, so I read a bunch of his books and found that the tone spoke to me very directly, that it really fit with how I saw the world and what entertained and amused me in a story.

What attracted you to Get Shorty *as a property to make yourself?*

DH: MGM brought it to me. I didn't know they were looking to develop it. At the time, I had just over-committed myself. I was trying to be smart about my life, so I thought, "Okay, I just have to bite the bullet and pass on this." So I told my agent I just didn't have time. About ten minutes later I thought, "I just made a huge mistake!" So I called back and said, "How about this? Just tell them I desperately want to do it, and ask them how long they can wait." It took almost two years before I got to it. But the whole time, while I was working on everything else, I kept thinking, "Oh man, *Get Shorty* is the one. I wish I could just do that." And then when I got to it, it was so much fun working on it that I thought, "Boy, this has to be a good sign. I couldn't be enjoying myself more, just spending the day laughing out loud with the people I was working with." And it turned out I was right—it was a good sign.

When MGM first brought the project to you, was it just a straight adaptation of the novel, or did they already have this idea to create something completely different?

DH: No. They just said, "Make the movie/book into a TV show." When I went in my first pitch was just, "Hey, let's reinvent it. Let's start over. Let's have new character names but keep the premise." I think the idea of the story and Leonard's tone as it pertained to *Get Shorty*, in most people's minds, had gotten tied up with Barry Sonnenfeld. He did a wonderful job with that movie, but he kind of changed some primary colors in that film. There's a way to ground it in a sensibility that I feel more when I read Leonard's stuff than I do in watching that movie.

Leonard's not around and he's not producing right now, but I think he would probably really gravitate towards this. I don't want to presume to speak for him but I wouldn't be surprised if he wouldn't at least partially get excited about his work being done in a more grounded, grittier way. And not losing the irony. Not losing the vulnerability. Tough guys who have frailties and vulnerabilities and just have a human side to them can be a source of real pathos that goes beyond just being a funny gag and become something moving. Those are all elements that, while captured in the Sonnenfeld's version of the movie, also lend themselves to a more contemporary, grounded execution.

What kind of reaction have you gotten from the original fan base? Were people initially angry about your reimagining the story?

DH: Yeah. Before the show came out I could already tell there was a palpable skepticism among the critics. And to be honest, I don't think we initially did a great job publicizing the show in terms of setting up expectations that this was really going to be something different. I spent a lot of time trying to say that to critics. Sure enough, our reviews were divided into people who loved the show and were delighted and immediately clocked that it was its own beast, and those who seemed to think we had failed to copy the movie, which they'd been expecting. They were like, "This isn't the movie, you failed at that." Those people missed the boat completely. But then those people stopped watching and the response we've been getting moving forward has been fantastic.

I've worked with Barry Sonnenfeld on *Pushing Daisies* and I think he's terribly talented, but the truth is, as sensibilities have evolved, I think people were ready for a new reincarnation of the story.

In the past you've said that Leonard's being so revered made the series an intimidating challenge. Would you like to talk about that?

DH: Because I've always felt that his sensibility was so sympatico with my taste, I wasn't terribly worried. He was so formative for me that I felt the best thing to do was to put that out of my head and just enjoy this whole thing as much as possible. And that's what I did. Occasionally I'll check back in with Leonard and think about how he would do this, or I'll remember bits of his story or details that were so wonderful. Certainly I made a list of the things we all loved about the book. But then you gotta let the ideas fly and trust that there's enough compatibility there between who I am and who Leonard was.

In the series you made the decision to focus on the drug cartels rather than the mob. What were some of the considerations that went into that specific change?

DH: It was a grounding thing and a way to get away from some of the tropes that have become more thoroughly explored since Leonard wrote the book and are now very recognizable, in terms of the films. Cosa Nostra isn't around anymore. They don't really exist. I'm sure there's Italian crime, but the classic mob no longer exists, at least as far as I know. You do have organized crime, but the biggest source of organized crime that we feel here in California comes from south of the border. And that's got its own trope. There are clichés there as well, but it was a good place to start to ground it. That was the first decision.

And we looked at having Miles as a Latino actor. One of the first serious casting conversations I had was to make an offer to a Latino actor. That went south. He and I didn't see eye to eye about the show, so it didn't work out. Then someone hit on the idea of Chris [O'Dowd] and Chris doing it with an Irish accent, and I was like, "Great! That's wonderful!" We were just looking for ways to reinvent it without departing from Leonard's tone.

How much fun has it been for you to work with Miles, a character who is an antihero, and trying to show him as a relatable, regular person who also then does the bad things he does?

DH: It's a blast because immediately you have that conflict in the juxtaposition of somebody with real emotions and real wants and needs and frailties, which makes them sympathetic, and yet they have an existence which in some ways can be considered sociopathic or, at least antisocial. That immediately gives you something enormously fun to work with. As characters get darker and darker, it becomes tricky. You start seeing them more from the outside and they become less sympathetic. If you see the journey that Tony Soprano took later in the series, or Walter White took later in *Breaking Bad*…. Trading in the sympathy of the audience for the fascination the audience has with watching that evolution. We're calibrating that same challenge right now in season three as Miles gets a little darker and a little further on his journey. I think he's still fascinating but less sympathetic, and that's a tricky line to walk.

You mentioned The Sopranos. *Your series has a similar tone. I know* Get Shorty *is supposed to be more of a comedy, but they feel quite similar. Was that intentional? Was* The Sopranos *an inspiration?*

DH: *The Sopranos* was life changing for me. I wasn't really drawn to television until I saw *The Sopranos*. It changed everything. I was a real snooty, wannabe playwright. And then I saw *The Sopranos* and realized this was better than anything I was going to see in Manhattan. It absolutely turned me around. So yeah, it's been the standard. I'd say it's the bar. It's not a coincidence that we brought Allen Coulter from *The Sopranos* to direct the pilot.

And you've got Peter Bogdanovich!

DH: And we've got Peter Bogdanovich. [Laughs.] And [screenwriter] Terry Winter is a friend of mine and I love his sensibility and his work. Those guys.... There's part of my brain that always hears their voices.

You reference Chili Palmer in the series, which I think is funny.

DH: It's pretty subtle and it's a tiny reference. In the first episode Miles is driving on to the lot and they stop him. They won't let him on the lot. And they wave someone else through and say, "Morning, Mr. Palmer," and you get a glimpse of some guy who's vaguely Travolta-like.

Even the meaning of the title Get Shorty *changes in the series.*

DH: The studio kept asking me what "Shorty" stood for. Who was Shorty? We kicked around a couple of ideas. One of them was his daughter, which I think I pitched initially and then I said, "That's a dumb idea." And they said, "Oh, we love that!" They really loved that. I got on my high horse and said, "No, no, no, no, I'll find something." And then when we got to the very end of the pilot, having him say "love you, shorty" was immediately moving to me! And I thought, "Oh no, they were right." [Laughs.] That's exactly what Shorty meant.

One of my favorite changes you made was having the film they're making be a Merchant Ivory type of film instead of a B-movie.

DH: Again, it's just about juxtaposing. The heart of this story and premise is juxtaposing these unlikely, uncultured thugs with ostensibly glamorous world of Hollywood. And then the thugs quickly realize, "Oh, this is not so different from us." Those funny culture clashes are really what fuel it—taking characters who are so different and putting them in the same room together. By that token, it felt like putting something as culturally different as possible to the sensibilities of these characters would be the funniest. So giving them a Merchant Ivory film and having them all sit around and talk about the story.... There's also something oddly moving about watching characters who are so unlikely actually get invested in a film or story that's so different and them actually crawling into it saying, "Oh no, she's broken hearted...." I find it sort of a testament to the power of story.

And then, not to mention the fact that *The Sopranos* had done that.

Christopher Moltisanti went and made a crappy horror movie. It was funny, but we wanted to make sure we were going in a very different direction.

Let's talk about Chris O'Dowd. He's especially terrific in this role. What do you think he brings to the character that other actors might not have?

DH: First of all, we got very lucky with this group in that they all are very funny but have real dramatic chops as well. Chris can do both at the same time. He can play a very serious scene and ground it, and yet some little part of him is always looking for, where's the irony, where's the humor? In fact, if you keep the humor away from him for too long, he'll come to you and say, "Come on!" It's like flying. For somebody that's that funny, the feeling they get is such a high that if they're deprived of it they start getting itchy. He's able to do both and he really hungers to do both.

Sean Bridgers' role as Louis grows as the series progresses. Did you know from the very beginning how substantial his part would be, or did that grow as you were writing?

DH: We knew his character was going to be big, but we didn't know at all what the character type would be. We went back and added the fact that he was a Mormon later. I didn't even pitch that. That was one of my writers. Then we held auditions. We got very close to casting somebody who was a little more what you'd expect. He was a very good, very funny Italian actor who was kind of what I'd imagined. But then Sean came in and had this whole wonderful, different take on the thing and just made it his own. We all said, "Let's do that." What a great original way to go.

You mentioned the decision to make him a Mormon. There is a lot of talk in the series about "soaking" [a technicality allowing a Mormon man to insert his penis into a woman outside of matrimony as long as he doesn't move it around]. Did you already know about soaking, or was this something you discovered while you were writing?

DH: One of the writers in the room had heard about this from somebody. I still don't know how true it is, but I believe there's some reality in Mormon kids finding a way around the rules. [Laughs.] But it's not a firsthand anecdote.

I read that people were initially surprised by your casting Ray Romano. As we both know, he'd done some more dramatic stuff, but people always seem to see him as a sitcom actor. But he's absolutely terrific in Get Shorty.

DH: I went and spent time with Terry Winter just before he got *Vinyl* going. When I left I thought, "It's a shame I'm not going to work with Ray Romano. He's going to be so great in this." Because I'd seen what he did in the pilot and I'd thought, "What an interesting actor and what an interesting way to reinvent himself."

Ray is the nicest guy in the world. He really is that nice and sweet. But he really is hungry to do some serious acting. When I met with him about *Get Shorty* I said, "I do want this to be funny." And he said, "Yeah, that comes with the model. Don't worry about that!" But what he meant was, "I don't want to do sitcom stuff anymore. I want to go darker." His friend Brad Garrett had just done a turn on *Fargo*, and I think Ray saw that and thought, "Yeah, I can do something like that!" So I said, "This is that. This is what that is."

Occasionally he'll ask a question, but what he's saying is, "Is there a way through this scene that goes deeper than just funny? Is there a way to find some real emotion, some real tragedy, something to make sure it's believable?" He's fantastic and he manages to do exactly what we're trying to do with the show.

At this point, how far do you envision the series going?

DH: I don't know that this is a ten season show, but I think we could go on for a bit. The challenges are that Epix is hard to get and find, and that affects foreign sales. So there are challenges that go even beyond how many viewers we get. I'm hoping that isn't what dictates when we end the show. But creatively, I think Miles becomes less of a fish out of water, so the premise changes and the dynamic changes. But the collision of crime and making movies, we could get a few more years out of this.

What has been the single most pleasant surprise you've encountered while working on the show?

DH: There's something so fun about this show that everybody, I believe, has a great time. I've done this enough now that you can have a great time and end up with crummy work. More commonly, you can have a really lousy time and the work turns out great, but it's such a painful process. To have a premise, and I really credit Leonard with this, that he came up with a story that's so fun at its heart and that's dark and yet gives us a fairly optimistic view of humanity. You kind of love these bad guys. You feel for them and love them. They're fun to be around. It's a fun world to live in. Even the darkness is fun, and that's contagious. On top of that, we got lucky with our group of people. We were very lucky to have the actors and crew that we have. There's a lot of pressure involved in making a TV show, and there are a lot of aspects that aren't so much fun. So when the group of people is really having a good time, you know you're lucky and you want to hold on to that experience.

9

Jane Jones

Jane Jones (formerly Leonard) was born in 1950, the oldest of Elmore Leonard's five children. She attended Catholic school and then attended Grand Valley State College. While there, she found that college wasn't for her and left the school. "My parents weren't upset," she recalls. "They were probably glad because they didn't have to pay tuition." She then worked in retail for a number of years, managing a clothing store. After that, she went to work as an assistant to her father, typing up his manuscripts. She would end up typing his novels for the rest of her father's life.

She also worked with her brother, Peter, at the advertising agency Leonard, Mayer, and Tocco. She would work there for thirty years. During that time, the small firm handled such notable accounts as Volkswagen and Audi. As a hobby/side job, she and a friend obtained their builders licenses and went into housing renovation. The two would pitch their fathers to help them purchase houses in upscale neighborhoods. Then Jones and her friend/partner would dramatically renovate them, reselling them for a tidy profit and paying their fathers back with interest.

Today she is working as an interior designer. In addition, she works with her sister, Katy, and her sister-in-law, Julie, doing staging for realtors. Although Jane Jones' father has been gone for nearly a decade now, it's clear that he left his mark on her; during correspondence regarding this interview, she used an exclamation point and then wrote in parentheses "Elmore hated exclamation points."

ANDREW J. RAUSCH: *What kind of father was Elmore Leonard?*

JANE JONES: Great! [Laughs.] He was the greatest father. He was always fun. When we were really little kids we'd always want to go to the grocery store with him because he'd always buy us gum. And he would play with us. This was when we were still living in Lathrup Village. We would play this game called "guns." He started it. I think I was around ten or eleven. It was me, Peter.... Christopher was probably part of it, but he was just a little kid. Everyone had a toy gun and we'd take turns. It was like hide and seek with guns. When you found the person, you'd go "bang!" or something and the person who got shot would fall dead! [Laughs.] We played that game so many times. It was my dad's game and we'd play it with him.

Did he get really into it? Did he flop over and play dead?
JJ: Oh my gosh, yes! Absolutely.

Guns always played a significant role in his writing, so it's interesting that this was the game he'd play with you.
JJ: Yeah. The story is that when he was in the fifth grade, he wrote a story about a war. It might have been World War I or something. I guess it wasn't a story, but a play that they acted out in his classroom. There must have been guns involved there. But he wasn't a gun person at all. He didn't own guns.

So, that game was fun. He was always a fun dad.

Elmore loved watching baseball. Did you go to a lot of Tigers games when you were growing up?
JJ: Tons. I remember for a time his mother lived with us. I have memories of going to Tigers Stadium with him and his mom and probably Peter. I would do the score card, filling in the hits and the outs. He taught me how to do that, and I thought that was the coolest thing. I couldn't do it today. I don't even know if they still have score cards today.

My parents got divorced in 1976 and then he married Joan, and she died, and then he married Christine. But anytime we would go to see him in the summer, we always played baseball or volleyball. And he would play whiffle ball with us. Everyone would play and that was fun. He was like a kid.

After your parents were divorced in 1976, did your father change in any way?
JJ: No. When he married Joan, she was very much into his work. Very interested and very involved. I think she helped him write from the woman's point of view.

We loved our mom and our dad. When they got divorced, it didn't change anything with us in how we felt about him. He was still our dad.

Our fun dad. And our mom was still our mom. We just didn't judge him. In fact, that was something that he had always taught us, just in general—don't be judgmental.

Did you ever have a sense as a child that your dad, as a published author, was doing something different from what other dads were doing?

JJ: No. Here's the thing, when we lived in Lathrup Village, we lived there from the time I was born in 1950 until we moved to Birmingham in 1963. When we lived in Lathrup Village, he'd go down to the basement before work and he'd write from five o'clock in the morning until eight o'clock when he had to leave for work. So I never really saw him writing. Then when we moved, he had an office in downtown Birmingham. It was this little second floor, one-room place where he would write. And then he also did advertising for people. And he was also writing things for Encyclopædia Britannica. So he needed a place without the kids to go and work and have quiet.

Nobody I knew, even up to high school and college, knew him because he was not a name yet. Nobody would ever say, "Oh, your dad is Elmore Leonard?" They would have no idea who he was. He was just my dad. He was just my dad who on Saturdays had an electric frying pan and would make hamburgers with pumpernickel bread instead of a bun for any of my friends who was over. If they were over, they would get a hamburger.

You talked about Elmore not being a name back then. He had written for many, many years and then finally broke through in the mid–1980s, and then really became popular in the 1990s. What was it like to have been along for that journey and to finally see him achieve that level of success?

JJ: We just thought it was pretty cool. I remember one night at dinner we were sitting having dinner together, and.... The question in our family is who actually answered the phone, because everybody thinks it was them. But whoever did answer the phone—it was one of my brothers—and it was Clint Eastwood. [Laughs.] So he said, "Dad, Clint Eastwood is on the phone!" And it was in the days when you could unscrew the voice part of the phone so no one could hear you if you were trying to listen in on a phone call. We each ran into a different room and listened in on the phone call from Clint Eastwood. [Laughs.] Everything was exciting about it. We were thinking, "Our dad is writing and is famous." We just enjoyed it! And my brothers all seem to think that they were the one who answered the phone.

When *Stick* (1985) was being filmed, my dad took us all to Florida. Another time he took my sister, Katy, to Arizona when they were filming something with Lee Majors. She fainted and Lee Majors gave her his bandana. She was mortified. [Laughs.] We met George Clooney. That was super fun. He had a party after *Out of Sight* (1998) and had most of the cast and crew come over. My daughter Shannon was home from Chicago, and she never left his side. Then when he'd finish a drink, she'd say, "Oh, would you like another drink?" It was vodka and cranberry. And he'd say, "Yeah, sure!" And from this day on, we call that drink a Clooney. [Laughs.] She was so hung over the next day and I had to take her to the airport. I'll never forget this. She was so happy she got to stand next to George Clooney. That was fun.

The one thing that I missed that was a huge thing was the time Aerosmith came to his pool. I was in Chicago with my daughter. I was so mad. [Laughs.]

Elmore not only listened to jazz, but listened to rock as well. To think of him in his eighties wearing a Nine Inch Nails shirt is just fantastic. I think that also gives some indicator as to how he was still able to write like a young man when he was older. When you were growing up, was there ever an overlap between the music you listened to and the music Elmore listened to?

JJ: He *loved* Willie Nelson. He took all of us to a Willie Nelson concert one time when they came to Detroit. He liked Steely Dan. My sister Katy was like, "Why would he like Steely Dan?" [Laughs.] But he loved, loved, loved Willie Nelson. So at my dad's funeral, on the altar, this amazing violinist we had played a solo of one of his songs on the violin. It was the most moving thing. There was just silence. That was in his honor because she knew my dad and loved him and knew he liked that song.

Out of all the memories you have of your father, do you have a favorite?

JJ: One of my favorite memories is him writing a scene in a book just because he knew it would make me gag. I think it was in *Be Cool*, and I think the scene took place at Carmine's in LA. Somebody is having lunch with this record producer. The producer ordered his lunch and part of it was coleslaw. He was eating coleslaw and chewing with his mouth open, and it was in the corners of his mouth and the guy he was with was quietly gagging and couldn't even stand looking at this. I called my dad and said, "Oh my God, what in the world are you doing?

I'm gagging!" And he said, "I knew you would. I put that in there for you." [Laughs.] I love the thought that he was writing this book and he thought, "I'm going to make Jane gag."

You spent a lot of years typing up his novels. How did that come about?

JJ: I couldn't do the job I had anymore because I had this sciatic nerve problem. So all I could do was sit around. He knew that. Maybe it was his secretary or somebody had moved on. He always wrote his books on plain lined yellow paper. He would cross words out and make notes. This was when you took typing in class in high school, so I said sure I'd come do that for him. He paid me something like five cents a word. Some unbelievably small amount. [Laughs.] This was when you used a typewriter and you had to put in carbon paper. And you could hardly erase because it would smear. And then I typed up until his last book, which he had started but didn't finish.

What do you remember about that book?

JJ: *Blue Dreams.* I actually don't remember much about it. It's kind of gone out of my mind. It was the last thing, and it was such a.... I don't know. We had a lot of talk about, "Should Peter finish it? What should we do about it?" But we never did. I don't think we will.

One thing I do remember is him finding the *Charlie Martz* [previously unpublished] short stories. I think he found them in his basement. I don't know how it all came to be, but he called me and I came over there and he said, "Can you type these for me?" So I did. I called him and said, "Oh, my God! I love these!" I said, "Should you make these into a book?" And what he would always just say was just "yeah?" and look at you with that smirky smile. And I said, "Yeah. I just love them." So we did end up doing that. Because we thought it was good because you could see how his writing started in the fifties and then how much better it got.

What else do you remember about typing up his books? Would you two have conversations about the writing itself?

JJ: He'd kill off a character. Then I'd be typing and call him up. "Why'd you do that?" "Well, I couldn't make her talk" or something like that. I would question him on things, and then when he'd end a book, I'd always tell him what I thought. And I said after every one, "This is your best one ever." He laughed at that all the time. I knew what was going on in the books as he was writing them, and that was fun.

And you know what? I've never read any of his books in actual book form. Maybe I'll start.

How many pages of the book would he give you at a time? And were the pages completely finished when he gave them to you, or would he sometimes need to rewrite them?

JJ: He'd give me the first couple of chapters. Then as he was working, he'd maybe take those back and rewrite some things. When I would get the pages, it was on the yellow paper, but he'd typed it. He didn't give me his written pages. It was typed. But then, if he made changes, that was done by pen. And it was crossed out with things in the margins. Sometimes he'd add a page. He was always working on it while he was writing it. Or maybe he'd get a whole different idea or change a person's name. When he changed a person's name and you're typing it on the typewriter, it was the worst thing ever. You'd have to redo every page! Basically you're redoing what you just did. But he was always just trying to make it be the best it could be.

Were there ever any things in his writing that he asked you for your opinion on? Or did you ever say anything to him that resulted in him making story changes?

JJ: No, I don't think so.

It's common for writers to incorporate details from real life into their work. Did you ever recognize any elements of things from his real like in his work?

JJ: Not that I can think of.

Did you ever see an aspects of any Elmore's characters that reminded you of him?

JJ: All of them! All of the guys. The main characters, I think, were all him.

Are there any specific traits of Elmore that would stand out in his characters where you were like, "That's him"? Or a recurring trait that reminded you of him?

JJ: I think the thing is, with his characters, even if it was a bad guy, he was a nice guy. My dad would say, "Even bad guys would sit down and have a bowl of cereal in the morning." They're not necessarily bad people, but they do bad things.

9. Jane Jones

They're normal people, but instead of working at the supermarket or working at the school—

JJ: They're robbing banks. And they're nice to their moms.

Did you ever see any changes in Elmore's work that you felt resulted from things happening in his life? Like him sobering up or things like that?

JJ: I think he had a little bit of a harder time with his stories, and also a couple of times he quit smoking. He quickly found out that he couldn't quit smoking and write. He had to be smoking his Virginia Slims. I think that maybe when he was going through AA and all that, I think maybe he was a little bit slower. But I don't think it changed his writing. It just seemed like it was taking a little longer.

Were there any scenes or novels that you remember Elmore being particularly proud of?

JJ: I don't think there were any that he didn't feel that way about. And then as soon as he would finish, he would just move on to the next one. He'd take a few weeks off and we'd go to his pool and play baseball. But other than that, he was head down, writing. He really loved doing it.

You mentioned him smoking Virginia Slims. It's funny because he always wrote these very macho characters who would probably never smoke Virginia Slims.

JJ: Menthols. The real long ones. Yeah, I know. We used to kid him about it.

Once Elmore achieved the tremendous level of success he did, did he change at all?

JJ: Absolutely no change. I'd go over there and pick up something or just visit him, and he'd be sitting at his desk in a t-shirt with holes in it. He'd stop and talk to me. He was not at all affected by success. Not. At. All. He was just the most regular guy you could ever meet. Just an average guy who wore glasses. If you looked at him, you'd think, are you really a famous writer?

Do you have a favorite of your father's novels, and if so why that one?

JJ: My favorite is *Get Shorty*. It was funny. I just liked it, but I can't explain why. I feel like I have to read them again because I haven't looked at *Get Shorty* since I was typing it. I remember the scenes in the movie, and I would say that one.

Perspectives on Elmore Leonard

You can't speak for Elmore, but do you think he had any regrets?

JJ: Maybe that he married Christine. [Laughs.] That was a huge, huge mistake.

What stands out in your mind about August 20, 2013, the day Elmore passed away?

JJ: Katy, Christopher, me, and Bill spent the night with him when he was in hospice. We had to set alarms and take turns giving him morphine. Two people were on a couch. I was on a blow-up bed with Christopher. We laughed. This is the night before he died. He would be making noises and Chris would go, "Dad! I'm trying to sleep!" And then we'd give him the morphine and we'd be like, "Oh my god, did we miss that last one?" It was surreal to be there doing that. We would laugh nervously. Then Chris would start singing "Don't Rock the Boat" because the air bed was wobbling back and forth. It seemed like a happy thing. And then that morning.... He died around 7:15 or something, and it was just like, whoa! You can't believe that it happened.

We laughed at so much after the funeral. We decided we were going to do a play on a funeral called *Funeral: The Musical*. And have a song that was "I'm Sorry for Your Loss" because that's what every single person said. Then my brother, Bill, put words to it to the music of "The Shadow of Your Smile." We laughed, and that's what my dad would have wanted. Not at his funeral, of course. But after while we were sitting outside of his house, having some drinks. It was nice. It was like, "This is how it should be."

What are your thoughts on Elmore's legacy today?

JJ: I'm happy that he's out there so much and that people are buying his books. I think that's great.

10

C. Courtney Joyner

In a writing career that has spanned nearly four decades, C. Courtney Joyner has worked in a variety of mediums, including screenwriting, novelist, and nonfiction writer/researcher. His first produced screenplay was the 1987 cult shocker *The Offspring (a.k.a. From a Whisper to a Scream)*, which he co-wrote with Darin Scott and director Jeff Burr. After that, he was off and running, knocking out screenplay after screenplay. His twenty-five produced screenplays include multiple installments in both the *Trancers* and *Puppet Master* franchises, as well as a handful of collaborations with director Mark L. Lester. In addition to his screenwriting, Joyner has also directed the films *Trancers III* (1992) and *Lurking Fear* (1994). He is a member of the Western Writers of America, the Horror Writers Association, and the International Thriller Writers.

As a novelist Joyner has written in other genres but he is best known for writing Westerns. He was nominated by the Western Fictioneers for their Peacemaker Award for his short story "The Two Bit Kill" from the anthology *Law of the Gun* (2007) and was nominated again for Best Short Story for "Christmas for Evangeline" in the collection *Six Guns and Slay Bells* (2012). He is the author of the Shotgun series, which includes the books *Shotgun* (2013), *The Bleeding Ground* (2016), *Bushwhacked: The John Bishop Shotgun Saga* (2017), and *These Violent Times* (2018). For *Shotgun* he was nominated for another Peacemaker Award, this time in the category of Best First Novel.

In addition to his credentials as a popular Western novelist, he is a noted Western historian who was the film/TV editor for *True West* magazine for three years and has contributed commentaries and documentaries to more than 100 Blu-ray releases. In 2009 he authored *The Westerners: Interviews with Actors, Directors, Writers, and Producers* where one of the writers interviewed was Elmore Leonard. Additionally, Joyner wrote the text for film director/photographer Steve Carver's photography collection, *Western Portraits: The Unsung Heroes & Villains of the Silver Screen* (2019).

ANDREW J. RAUSCH: *In your book* The Westerners *you write, "With every story published, Leonard was quietly influencing Western fiction." Do you want to talk about that?*

C. COURTNEY JOYNER: I think the big thing that was happening, when Leonard was breaking in with his short stories in the pulp magazines, was his different approach to plot and character.... Let me jump back a little bit for some context. In the earlier fifties, you have to remember that there was this explosion of Louis L'Amour because of his first novel, *Hondo* (1953). That had a weird history because he had written a short story ("The Gift of Cochise") that John Wayne's company bought and was expanded into the feature-length script by James Edward Grant, and then Wayne paid L'Amour to have the novel written as a tie-in to the film. L'Amour writes the novel, but now he's using James Edward Grant's script as his outline and the book's a big success. The point is that that formula, the giant on horseback in the buckskin suit who rides in to save the day, became this model of the L'Amour western hero which others followed. Whether it's *Hondo* or *The Sacketts* [book series] or on and on, these things were extraordinarily popular and very enduring, but his style kind of set a pattern for the way Westerns were being approached at the time.

And then suddenly, here comes Elmore Leonard. And it wasn't about some hero in a buckskin suit. It was about a farmer who needed money who's holding a shotgun on a guy, waiting for a train. ["3:10 to Yuma," 1953.] A whole different thing. The level of realism was different. By that, I don't mean that other Western writers had not written realistic fiction. Of course they did, but if E.L. wrote about a sheriff, he was a fellow trying to get through his day without being shot so he could get home to his wife and kids. He wasn't myth building, which a lot of Western fiction at the time—L'Amour and those guys—were doing. He was not. His was about ordinary people in extraordinary circumstances. He did it so beautifully and then slowly, I think it spread to other writers. They didn't imitate his style, as far as his verbiage and that type of thing. But I think certain writers, like Frank O'Rourke for example, who's a great favorite of mine, I think he was influenced. It was an interesting little revolution that happened because it was going against the idea that someone larger than life had to be the center of Western stories. Elmore Leonard was saying, "No, life is enough."

96

I'm no Western expert but it seems to me that not only did he not do any hero building but that he also wrote about more anti-hero characters than his contemporaries. It seems like there was at least more of a gray area morality within his characters than what had come before in things like Gunsmoke. *Do you think that's true?*

C.C.J.: You're looking at both sides of the coin. In the old half-an-hour black-and-white days *Gunsmoke* used to start with Matt Dillon on Boot Hill talking about the latest guy that he killed. A lot of these shows were the ones derived from the radio show, and Sam Peckinpah wrote a number of those episodes. Very bleak stuff at the same time E.L. was breaking through the short-story market. Later, in the color shows, they made Matt a little bit more of a clean-and-scrubbed hero character. That came later. Early on he was more of a murky type of personality and someone who carried a lot of guilt with him. I think that was also part of what Elmore Leonard was doing, and I'm sure the early *Gunsmoke* writers were paying attention to the Westerns in the magazines, as that's where the studios discovered E.L. for the movies. The violence that we would normally see in Western TV shows from that early era was different. It felt very clean and formalized. Sergio Leone had a wonderful time exaggerating it. With Elmore Leonard violence could be random or a mistake, and it carried circumstances. And it wasn't always clearly motivated. It was just the way people behaved. Again, that was just not the type of thing you saw generally, certainly not in the pulp Westerns or the formula stuff and that was a part of the publishing world E.L. was existing in. He was a short-story writer who was bucking trends. Before *The Tall T*, E.L. had one of his stories ("Moment of Vengeance") produced on *Schlitz Playhouse*, and all the problems he had with TV westerns fell into place. He told me, "Gene Nelson was the good guy and he was a tap dancer, so it looked like he was going to go into a dance instead of drawing his guns. The TV westerns all had a gunfight, two guys facing each other in the street, and according to my research that never happened. If you wanted to shoot somebody, you go into the saloon where they're having a drink and you shoot him, turn around and leave. I never did have two guys facing each other in any of my work."

Several of his Western novels feature minorities as protagonists. I know there had been some stuff before him that had minorities but he was now making them primary characters. He focused on Apaches, Black characters, there was Bob Valdez [from Valdez Is Coming, *1970] who was*

Mexican-American. My guess is that that there weren't many Western writers doing this before him. Is that right?

C.C.J.: I think this was something he wanted to explore because he wanted to show more of the multicultural existence of the West. I think you're right but certainly there were other writers going back to Zane Grey that featured characters who were different nationalities; Germans in the West, Swedes in the West and what have you. Jack Shaeffer's *Shane* (1949) does this beautifully, but they didn't create quite the tapestry that Elmore Leonard was creating. The homesteads that others wrote about tended to be these perfect places, welcoming to everyone, until the bad man rode in and had to be dealt with. That's not what E.L. was doing with his settings, his border towns, with his non-white characters. One of the more interesting things that goes right to this, you mentioned Bob Valdez—this is also true in *Hombre*—was the introduction of non-white characters who were policemen and constables in the West, and faced prejudice. In *Valdez Is Coming*, Bob Valdez is seen as the guy who keeps the Mexicans in line in this small town, but has no real authority with the ranchers, until he pushes them. They come back at him because no Mexican constable is going to be an upstart, or defy their power. Then, Valdez starts his vendetta. Of course, in *Hombre* there's the wonderful moment in the movie where Fredric March says to Newman that you have to be an Apache to be a constable on the reservation. Newman doesn't respond, but that's when everyone knows that the Apache sitting with them is the law. It's a great moment in the movie, but of course the novel is written from an entirely different point of view than the film adaptation, but carries the same impact because of the white character's reactions to being dependent on an Indian for their safety.

E.L. would always do deep research. As you know, he would just devour magazines, anything, for information, especially when it came to things like the lives of the Apache, or life in a territorial prison. When he found a nugget of something, like the status of a lawman from an Indian reservation, he'd run with it in his story instead of making the character the usual tall man with a badge, which I don't think he found very interesting.

Do you remember the first Elmore Leonard book you read?

C.C.J.: I believe the very first Elmore Leonard book I ever read was *Valdez Is Coming*.

Do you remember how that struck you at the time? Did it stand out from other Westerns you had read?

C.C.J.: Absolutely! I think it's tremendous. I bought the Gold Medal paperback, which had an unbelievable painting of Bob Valdez being crucified on the cover. That was the thing that caught my eye. I was probably twelve or thirteen years old. And I'm sure this had a big impact on me—Elmore Leonard was the very first Western novelist I ever read! I backtracked to read Jack Schaefer's *Shane* (1949) which my father had a copy of. I became a big fan of Frank O'Rourke's because I found the movie tie-in to *The Professionals* and also Donald Hamilton's *The Big Country* just knocked me out. I thought it was so cool that the guy who wrote Matt Helm also wrote Westerns. But I always drifted back to Leonard because he was the first Western author I ever read, really the first "adult" author I ever read, and had such a huge impact.

Do you have a favorite Leonard work?
C.C.J.: There's so much that's so great. I love *Valdez* because it's so damn readable, the language has its own rhythm, but when we're talking about Leonard westerns, *Hombre* is in its own class. One of the best Westerns ever written. After the Westerns, and he hit his crime-stride, all of those novels—that whole group... [*City Primeval:*] *High Noon in Detroit* (1980) is just tremendous. I really liked *52 Pickup* (1974), and didn't mind that the movie re-set it in L.A. Again, that was about regular people who get involved in a situation that just explodes all over them. And I don't think the Atlantic City series gets enough credit because I thought *Bandits* (1987) was great.

You're right. People don't talk about those novels quite as much.
C.C.J.: No, they don't. It's always either Florida or Detroit. And there was so much that was coming out—*Stick* (1983) and *Gold Coast* (1980), great books that were all kind of piling up on one another. I dog-eared [*City Primeval:*] *High Noon in Detroit* to death. I just thought it had the perfect sense of place and purpose.

Oh, and I also loved *Out of Sight* (1996). My favorites don't stop, do they?

You've mentioned a couple of Leonard's Westerns. Which of them is your favorite?
C.C.J.: Beyond *Valdez* and *Hombre*, which were life-changers, a Leonard Western that doesn't get anywhere near the literary credit it deserves is *Last Stand at Saber River* (1959). I think that's quite good. Back to *Hombre*, because that's its own animal. I have to take a deep

breath before reading it again, as I try to once a year, because it's a masterwork. Truly one of the best Westerns ever written by anyone, with great points about race. People pick up *Hombre* and expect the Paul Newman movie and then realize the novel is written from the point of view of the character Martin Balsam plays in the movie! *Hombre* is one of Leonard's few first-person books, so he was exploring new sides of his own technique, but in a totally unpretentious way which is the key to the book's greatness. Like the Apache-raised John Russell, the book is what it is and you can take the writing or leave it on its own terms. It's like the book itself is as tough as its characters. There are no tears here, no time for pity as you turn the pages.

Forty Lashes Less One (1972) is special because E.L. doesn't really adhere to his own famous ten rules of writing here. I think it's a beautifully written book but it's a denser style. I love the fact that he would play with his own work in that way, and here the issues of race in the West, in this case an actual race, and how the white and non-white characters deal with each other, is front and center.

I'm too young to have gotten into the original short stories until after they were collected—stories like "Three-Ten to Yuma" (1953), "The Captives" (1955), and "The Tonto Woman" (1998), which were all made into movies. I also really liked "The Big Hunt," and "The Kid."

Speaking of the short stories, Leonard's "Man with the Iron Arm" (1956), which is about a one-armed cowboy, is a precursor to your own Shotgun series. Was that story an inspiration?

C.C.J.: I wish I could say that it was. I probably would've written mine a little bit better. I didn't discover that story until recently and I was like, *holy cow!* I really do wish I had taken a look at that before for further inspiration, or lots of homages! But that one came a little bit late to me.

It's interesting how frequently those kinds of things occur. It supports the old adage that there is nothing new under the sun.

C.C.J.: When I was first writing *Nemo Rising* (novel version, 2018) as a spec TV pilot, it was at the same time *League of Extraordinary Gentlemen* (1999) hit the newsstands. A friend of mine told me about it and I said, "Nope! No, no, no. I do not want to know." I stayed very far away from it except that I did go see the movie [*League of Extraordinary Gentlemen*, 2003]. The thing was written and it was being circulated around. I think when you find out about these things it's better to stay away and often, you find out later, even if something is basically along the same lines, each individual takes on different approaches and they very rarely collide.

You wrote an article in True West *magazine in which you said you had saved all of Elmore Leonard's phone messages. Is that true?*
C.C.J.: Absolutely.

How did that interview come to pass, and what was the experience like?
C.C.J.: He was terrific! When I was finishing off *The Westerners*, I was very, very pleased with all the interviews I'd collected for it. Things like my talk with Warren Oates, that happened in college. Warren died before I even graduated. I was very lucky because I had gotten to go forward with these different folks. I thought I had really assembled a good group of talks, and everyone was so generous to me and many became friends. But McFarland wanted one more big interview in there to make the book marketable.

I really wanted Elmore Leonard. I got his address, and I can't remember how. I Googled it or something. I wrote him a letter and I explained what I was doing and who else I had spoken to. I made a point to mention Burt Kennedy because Burt had written the adaptation [of "The Captives"] for *The Tall T* (1957). A few weeks passed and I was with my girlfriend and there was a phone message for me. I'm so glad I ended up recording it and I didn't pick up the phone. He said, "Hey, I got your letter. I'd be happy to help you. I love Westerns. Let's do this." I didn't have to dog him. I didn't have to do anything except contact him and ask him if he'd help, and boy, did he!

I read that he had to put the interview off for a bit because he was trying to finish a chapter.
C.C.J.: That's true, he did. He was working on *Djibouti* (2010), the book about pirates in Somalia. We hadn't set the time, I remember this. I called him the day before because I had no idea when he wanted to do it and I didn't have an email address for him. He was really annoyed I called him, and I told him why I called and he was fine. He said, "I'll call you, don't worry about it."

The next morning he called me. He had been shoveling snow that morning. He was telling me about that. I think he felt bad he had gotten a little snappy, so he started to read his chapter to me over the phone! I kept thinking, I'm recording this. I didn't want him to think I was going to release an unauthorized chapter to the world! He was very excited that he had gotten to that point. I think there was a hump he needed to get over. He was very focused on that chapter and he had gotten over it. He was very pleased about that.

He was forthcoming and very honest. I had to edit the interview down because we talked for quite a while. After the book came out, there was a post about it on his website. He even mentioned it in an interview once! He was just wonderful about that. He talked about the ups and downs, particularly with the Westerns, and how that made him want to write the screenplays. That was the biggest shift in his life—him being able to be the voice of his own work on screen. It's there in the interview—the situation he had with *Hombre* where the difference in what he was paid and what Irving Ravetch and Harriet Frank, Jr., were paid to adapt it. Those are things that led to his original scripts like *Joe Kidd* (1972) and his scripting *High Noon, Part II* (1980), which was not very good. I think part of the reason is Lee Majors, but E.L. also thought director Jerry Jameson had done a poor job. It's just not good, and E.L. knew it, but he was very pleased he got to introduce his kids to The Six Million Dollar Man! Then later on, of course, he created *Desperado* (1987).

What do you think about Desperado?

C.C.J.: That was for Walter Mirisch and Universal, and was directed by Virgil Vogel who I was working with at the time. In fact, I saw Virgil's director's cut. I think the first one is fine. It's a very solid TV Western with an excellent cast, a very good concept and it's well-made. After *Centennial* and *The Big Valley* and all the rest, who better to direct a TV Western than Virgil? If *Desperado* had been a big mini-series, it would've been a lot more expansive and served E.L. better. Instead, they did it as a lean little palliative movie. Chuck Sellier, who directed *Silent Night, Deadly Night* (1984) and ran Sun Classics Pictures, was the supervising producer and Universal's dictate was to do the films on a tight budget. Larry Cohen wrote a couple of them, and the sequels were just extremely serviceable programmers, really.

What is your favorite adaptation of an Elmore Leonard Western?

C.C.J.: *Hombre* is tremendous. It covers so many wonderful areas about race and attitudes and the violence that comes from that. Richard Boone was one of Elmore Leonard's favorite actors, and his performance is wonderful. The film is just so down-at-the-heels realistic. It's so parched. The movie is almost the perfect model of what E.L. valued in his own work, even though he didn't do the adaptation. I think it's wonderful.

For an expansive adaptation of "The Captives," *The Tall T* is terrific. And it has Richard Boone in his first Leonard role. E.L. really appreciated the way Burt Kennedy handled his story, and told me, "I really liked it because (Kennedy) stayed right with the story. There weren't any asides that I noticed. He stayed right with the dialogue, and Boone got that. He made his part." I love that short-story and the way [Budd] Boetticher and Burt were approaching those Westerns they were making with Randolph Scott. "The Captives" just fit in perfectly. The one right before *Tall T*, *Seven Men from Now* (1956) feels like an Elmore Leonard story, and that was an original of Kennedy's. It's very dry and matter of fact and realistic and worked so well, it opened the way for them to do all the rest with Randolph Scott, starting with *Tall T*, which I do think is the best of the Ranown Westerns from the '50s.

What Delmer Daves did with *3:10 to Yuma* was also wonderful. I think it's terrific. It's so surprising now when you see it! First of all, Glenn Ford is the bad guy. which surprised a lot of people considering his star status and good guy image. It's also very sexually explicit for the time. They got away with quite a bit in the scenes with Felicia Farr. I think that first group of Westerns derived from E.L.'s stories are all quite extraordinary. Really quality films, which is what Leonard wanted. He was always aiming for the movies with his stories.

E.L. had reservations about *Joe Kidd*, although he liked Clint Eastwood, and still remembered his kids listening in on the phone when Eastwood called him. He didn't care for the way [director] John Sturges included some elements from *The Magnificent Seven* (1960) that were never used, including plowing the train through Henry Bumstead's saloon set. He said, "No, that train was Sturges' idea, one of his out-takes from *The Magnificent Seven*. Another one was when Eastwood was up in the bell tower and dropped a pot and hit the guy in the head. It wasn't a good picture at all." I always thought that E.L. was too harsh about *Joe Kidd*, but he'd written something tougher, about the struggles of the Mexicans who're being kicked off their land, and Kidd caught up in the war. All that stuff is in the movie, but it's really an okay action picture, with some nice scenes which are fun, but that's it.

Last Stand at Saber River (1997), the TNT movie, was a very solid western, and Selleck is very good in it. E.L. thought they'd done a good job on that one, even though it's gotten a little bit lost in the shuffle when people look at his Western movies. Talking about Elmore Leonard Westerns, was there anything more wonderfully surprising than *Justified*?

Justified is very much a modern day Western. Everyone else saw that and pointed it out, but Leonard always denied that. What are your thoughts on that?

C.C.J.: I did articles about *Justified* for *True West*. What I find interesting is the major shift that they did with the Raylan Givens character, because when we first see Raylan Givens in *Pronto* (1993)—

He's more of a hick in Pronto.

C.C.J.: He's Sam Elliott, who ended up being one of the greatest villains the series ever had! In *Pronto*, Raylan wasn't the Raylan from the show. With *Justified* you have this transformation where they make him youthful, almost streamlined, and turn him into Timothy Olyphant. To me, that shift brings him even closer to a classic Western character; the way Tim always carried himself and the purposefulness of his body language. He's not a cowboy or rancher. Good lord, he's a gunfighter and every character acknowledges it. That's the essence. And there are moments—like in season three and that great episode, "Guy Walks Into a Bar"—and I was actually there on the set when they shot some of that episode, you could feel the gunfight tension in the scenes with Tim and Neal McDonough. Incredible. The man with the badge and Stetson against the twitchy psycho. Raylan has the line in the pilot, "You draw, I put you down." How many times did he say that throughout the show? That's the mantra of a gunfighter. The ties to the Western in *Justified* can't be denied.

You see it in some of Leonard's other modern crime novels too. Elements of the Western, even if not pronounced.

C.C.J.: Isn't that also going to the very basics of what we're talking about? In whatever era the stories are set Leonard never wanted to go to the black hat vs. white hat dynamic. People are more complicated than that, even outlaws, and it doesn't matter what time period. People are people and they make crazy choices, and E.L. wrote his criminals that way. If they had a plan, it often got screwed up and then it was panic time, and their violence could be panicked. If some guy's coming for you then you sneak up behind him and clobber him over the head or shoot him. You don't wait for him to draw or turn around. If he's in a car or on a horse, it doesn't matter. You try and defend yourself. Sometimes, when there was a gunfight in one of the crime novels, E.L. was able to slyly mock what he saw as standard clichés in old movies and TV, because in the Westerns he wrote he wouldn't have his characters doing something phony. It's great fun in *Justified* or "Fire in the Hole" to have Raylan challenge somebody old-style, because it seems so incongruous in a modern setting, but when the shooting starts, look out. In the books E.L.'s gun fights were fast, not a bunch of gory descriptions, and they were panicky and they were realistic. It didn't matter if it happened in the 1880s or the 1980s.

You touched on 3:10 to Yuma *a few minutes ago. What were your thoughts on the 2007 remake?*

C.C.J.: We talked about it. He thought it was a big, loud, fun, action movie but it wasn't his story. We both agreed that Peter Fonda was terrific in it. When they burn the stage coach with the passengers inside, that is rough stuff. I'd never seen that before. I thought, whoa!

But it was a movie about explosions, and we laughed at that moment at the end, with the whistling for a horse like Roy Rogers, was pretty stupid. But there was a lot of fun to be had. It had some elements of darkness and Russell Crowe was quite good. I thought Christian Bale was good too, thoughtful, but the whole film was jazzed up. I think that was how E.L. saw it, that his story had been turned it into a big, summer popcorn movie. And I'm sure the check was wonderful. Of course, the movie did very, very well.

I reprinted a story of yours called "Wire" in an anthology I edited last year [A Time for Violence, 2019]. *When you sent it to me you said, "This is what I think of as my Elmore Leonard story." Do you want to talk about that and Leonard's influence?*

C.C.J.: My whole thinking about that was when I was asked to contribute to The Western Fictioneers anthology, I wanted to write something about the Grass Wars. I couldn't come up with something immediately off the top of my head. Again, I like to scrounge around and find some interesting tidbit about some character or something obscure that led to something.

I wrote one story that's been anthologized a few times called "Two Bit Kill." It was in a collection called *The Law of the Gun* (2010). The basis for that was that I actually found a law that existed in post–Civil War times that banned immigrants from selling building supplies for reconstruction. It was really targeted at Jewish immigrants so their businesses would fail. [Abraham] Lincoln is the one who overturned it. But I thought, that's an interesting thing on the books, that people may not know about. So, I wrote this little story about anti–Semitism in the West.

With "Wire," I was really lost and I didn't know what I was going to write. There was a great Western writer named Dusty Richards, who'd written at least a hundred books. He and his wife were killed in a car accident, but he was just the nicest man. We had breakfast one morning and I told him what my problem was because I knew Dusty was a walking encyclopedia on this type of stuff—especially anything to do with cattle and John Chisum and the power the big ranchers had. We started talking about the fact that the Cattlemen's Association managed to get a law on the books that listed pliers as a deadly weapon. If you saw someone with a pair of pliers, you could kill them. That was to stop the cutting of fences. I said, "Oh my god, that's great!" Dusty's the one that told me about that and I took off from there. In a way, that was finding this little bit of gold that people aren't aware of, the way Elmore Leonard and Gregg Sutter would go treasure hunting through all this research, to dig deep for an unusual fact or situation and use that for a character or a concept for E.L.'s writings. That's such a great way to do it, and I absolutely had that in my mind when I wrote that story, to try—really try—and follow Elmore Leonard's example.

11

Joe R. Lansdale

Joe R. Lansdale has written nearly fifty novels and thirty short story collections in a variety of genres, including Western, horror, suspense, crime, and science fiction. He has also written chapbooks, comic book adaptations, and worked on *Batman: The Animated Series* (1992). Lansdale is perhaps best known for his offbeat Bram Stoker Award nominated novella *Bubba Ho-Tep* (1994). The novella, which depicts Elvis Presley and John F. Kennedy battling an undead mummy in a nursing home, was later adapted into a successful film by Don Coscarelli of *Phantasm* (1979) fame.

Despite working in a number of genres, Lansdale has proven himself a master of the crime genre. He is the author of the bestselling *Hap and Leonard* series, which (to date) includes thirteen novels (including a mosaic novel), five novellas, and four short story collections. The crime series, which focuses on the exploits of best friends and private investigators Hap Collins and Leonard Pine, was adapted into the popular Sundance television series starring James Purefoy and Michael K. Williams. Other noted Lansdale crime novels include *Cold in July* (1989), *Freezer Burn* (1999), and *More Better Deals* (2020).

Lansdale has won an impressive ten Bram Stoker Awards and has been nominated for another nine. He has also received the American Mystery Award, the Horror Critics Award, and the "Shot in the Dark" International Crime Writers Award. In 2011, he received the Bram Stoker Award for Lifetime Achievement and in 2012 he was inducted into the Texas Literary Hall of Fame. He has been nominated for the World Fantasy Award eleven times.

Similar to Leonard, Lansdale has written both crime and Western novels and writes fantastic dialogue.

ANDREW J. RAUSCH: *Do you remember the first Elmore Leonard book that you read?*

JOE R. LANSDALE: The very first book I remember reading by him was *Hombre* (1961). I read that and I thought, "Oh my god, this is not like so many of the little paperback Westerns I had been reading. This is a novel and it's unique. It certainly feels like a Western, but it feels like something bigger." It really caught me in a way that made me think differently. He and Brian Garfield did that. Garfield wrote a lot of Westerns that were under pen names or quickie Westerns, but he also wrote these really great Westerns like *Wild Times* (1978) and so on. So between the two of them, I began to look at Westerns differently. Then I went out and read *Valdez Is Coming* (1970), and I thought, "Wow, something unique is going on here!" Then I read *Forty Lashes Less One* (1972). I read every Western he had done. Then I jumped over to the crime novels. I believe the first crime novel I ever read by him was *Mr. Majestyk* (1974). And I loved it! I still think it's kind of underrated because it's such a simple novel. It's about a melon farmer who wants to get his watermelons to market and that starts the whole ball rolling. I loved it!

I love a lot of the things in the Leonard novels. One aspect that I really love is that a lot of his novels are generally about little people with little dreams that seem magnificent to them. That's what they want. They want these little things that are important to them because of where they are on the food chain, so to speak. So I jumped from reading that one to reading just everything. *52 Pickup* (1974).... Every novel that he had written, really, but I remember *52 Pickup* in particular; how pleased I was with that; how surprised I was with that. That was one of those where a guy actually had money. Rich, industrious, but he was still a blue-collar guy. That was interesting to me because that was the people I knew. *City Primeval* (1980), which was also called *High Noon in Detroit*. To me, this was a guy whose uniqueness in dialogue seemed to be influenced by George Higgins, who is one of my favorite dialogue writers. I know this for a fact, actually, because I met Dutch's son, Peter, recently and he mentioned that. I agree with that one hundred percent that George and his dad wrote fantastic dialogue. That was an influence on me, too, you know. Aside from just reading those books and enjoying them immensely, I come back to the other real reason the stuff hung me up was just the stuff I said before about little people with little dreams. I've always thought those were sometimes far more interesting to me than the guy that's going to rob Fort Knox. I kind of like the idea of the guys that are gonna rob the beauty parlor. That's what interests me.

Leonard never wrote "bad guy" protagonists as bad guys. They were just regular people who called their moms, paid their bills, and also robbed liquor stores.

11. Joe R. Lansdale

JRL: It's one of those things, and I may feel a little bit different than he does here, but it's one of those things that you can't look at them as bad guys because everybody's the hero of their own story. What I think is interesting is that those bad guys *are* bad guys, because no matter what they do, they still step over the line that is socially acceptable. Eventually they become bad guys in the general sense, but what I thought he meant was they weren't evil in the classic sort of mustache-twirling way. They had complex lives and, like you said, they called their moms and they had to worry about what they were going to be having for lunch next week and so on and so on.... So what I thought he did was he did people. And some of those people chose the wrong path, some chose the better path. But in the end, they were all just people.

I thought that one of his unique abilities was his ability to show that a lot of these characters, like the character in *Out of Sight* (1996) that's a thief, were people. Or like *Rum Punch* (1992), which became *Jackie Brown* (1997), which is a great film that I loved because it really is like an Elmore Leonard novel. It's so much like that book. The idea was this simple thing: Jackie was trying to make a little money, but she chose a bad way to do it. But she wasn't what you would call a giant mastermind, deadly criminal. She wasn't a Hannibal Lecter or anything. She was just this one person that stepped over the line, and that made her a criminal, but she still had these very human aspects, like everybody does. And even with Ordell, here was a guy just living the American dream, only his American dream was a little different from what other people thought. And that made it even a little more frightening in its own way, but it made him interesting. It made him unique. But I never felt like I wanted to be those guys. It felt like I was on the outside looking in a little bit.

I love those books, and I love the way he approached those books. I have to say he was one of my favorite writers of all time.

His characters like, say, Ordell Robbie, are capable of extreme violence, but they're also funny and clever in an everyday "they don't know they're funny" kind of way. And then that humor is punctuated by the violence that often rears its head rather abruptly.

JRL: That's a technique I've always admired and have used a lot myself. The thing is, the funniest stuff is when the people in it don't know it's funny. Mark Twain once said, "There's no humor in heaven," meaning just about everything that's humorous is generally based on somebody's embarrassment, discomfort, or pain. And when you really think about it, that's true. Humor is based on the negative sides. People say, "How do you balance humor and horror?" They're not that far apart. They're pretty much the same thing a lot of the time. It's how you look at it and how you lay it out. I think that these guys, when they're having these things happen to them, it's damn sure not funny to them. But to an observer, it is funny.

There are some similarities between your writing style and Leonard's. You both write different things, but there are similarities. You both have wild characters, snappy dialogue, a mixture of humor and violence. Sometimes the humor is used to make the violence more shocking. Do you consider him an influence?

JRL: I think I was already doing some of those things, but I think he taught me how to do them better. Robert Bloch was a big influence on me early on. Robert Bloch wrote *Psycho* (1959) and all these great short stories. I got to meet Bob and we came to be friends, at least kind of in a more general way. We were on our way to being much closer friends, but then he got ill and died. But I'd see him at conventions, and it got to where we knew each other and we would talk. I bought a story from him, with my friend, Rick Klaw, for *Weird Business* (1995), which was a comic book version of stories by a variety of writers. We exchanged a lot of postcards and things like that. He was a very funny guy who frequently wrote about very dark subjects. He wrote a lot of classic short stories. I re-read his short stories from time to time. So he was the guy who probably taught me that as much as anybody.

Prior to him, it was Mark Twain. Mark Twain did that. If you read [*The Adventures of*] *Huckleberry Finn* (1884), some of that stuff is so funny, but it's so damn dark. There's always been that chain of writers. There was Twain, there was Bloch, and Fred Brown ... there's a ton of them that I could name, but the ones I mentioned were the big influences on that. When I got to Elmore Leonard, I think it sort of solidified that with me. I felt like he was a kindred soul who was there ahead of me and could sure teach me some tricks. So I tried to learn them.

Elmore Leonard tended to write about locales he was familiar with. Detroit and Miami most of the time. Since most of your stories take place in East Texas, is that something you find kinship with him in? Does that play into the reasons why you like his work?

JRL: I'm sure it did. I never really thought about it that way, but I always felt that he knew the places of which he spoke. I don't have a hundred percent career of just writing about east Texas, but ninety-eight percent career is what I would say. That's the place I know. It's the people I know. I know how they talk. That's the thing, too—if you don't pay attention and you read [George V.] Higgins or you read Leonard or maybe even me, you think, "Oh, they've all got the same kind of thing." No, they don't! We all have a kind of dialogue that's natural and designed to represent the way most people really talk. At least, we give the *illusion* of how most people really talk. There is a difference because those locales do come out. If you look, they're very identifiable from the way the dialogue is written.

Today every writer is aware of Leonard's "10 Rules for Writing." The primary rule everyone always talks about is "leave out the things readers skip." You seem to write along those same lines. Why do you think it is that writers often believe they have to overwrite? Are six pages describing the room ever really needed?

JRL: We have a society in which more is more, instead of less is more. I think that has a lot to do with the nature of the writer too. There are some writers, like Faulkner, whom I really like. He was a really rich and ripe writer, and I would say he overwrote sometimes. He did a lot of stream of consciousness, which is something I've learned a lot from. I use it frequently. He was just a very different kind of writer.

I like Leonard's rules, but I'm not a big rule follower. I tend to agree with a lot of them. One I do disagree with is, I write about weather. Twain always said he didn't, but then he does. *Huckleberry Finn* has a flood in it. It's there. But I do think that most people don't write weather well. Probably James Lee Burke is one of the best examples of somebody who does it very well. I like to believe I do it quite well. And the weather for me is representational of the characters to some extent, but it also gets back to that question you asked earlier about writing where you're from. And where I'm from, weather is a constant. It changes a lot. It could be hot in the day, and then all of a sudden comes a giant rainstorm or a tornado; the weather can change dramatically in one day. Certainly, it can change through the seasons. We've got a lot of rain in East Texas. It's not a dry place by any means. In fact, it's more like Louisiana. It's tropical.

The first half of the *Hap and Leonard* show—the first season was filmed in Baton Rouge, and that looks like East Texas. There are certain aspects of it that are different, for sure. There are certain kinds of trees here and there that are different. But Louisiana and East Texas are

111

just a line in the dirt. As far as the way they look, we have a sort of tropical environment. To me, the weather one I don't agree with unless you do poor weather. Just saying "it rained"... that's not necessarily a good thing. And you can strip that stuff down so much. Like, there's a writer called Paul Cain who wrote *Fast One* (1949) and *Seven Slayers* (1955), and I thought his work was so dull because it was so flat and nothing but "This is what happened next. He got out of the car and walked down the street." But Elmore Leonard's work—it changed dramatically, I think, around the time of *Glitz* (1985)—Elmore Leonard's work has a kind of muscular poetry. I'm one of those who like his work straight across the board, but I actually like the works before *Glitz* better. I think that he became a lot more mannered as time went on. Like Ray Bradbury became a lot more mannered. Like Ernest Hemingway became a lot more mannered. But that didn't mean they were bad, it just meant it was different. I loved all of his works, but I really liked it before it was quite so mannered.

The rules that he has, I think, are flexible, I think, because even he didn't follow them completely. If you look at some of my early work, and I know this is true with some of his early work, we use things besides *said*. Both of us were very much "you use said and you move on." Use said and that's it. I'm still very much that way. In my early work and Leonard's early work, we both tried different things. There was a book [*Charlie Martz and Other Stories: The Unpublished Stories*, 2015] that his son edited and had published of his early work, and you can see he used things like *replied*, and that's because we were learning from pulp models. You learn as you go. Hemingway taught me a lot about how to write in a lean manner. I think that he's less interesting in some ways than someone like Leonard, who had a more humorous and poetic side. But Hemingway is kind of the king and the most influential writer of the 20th century. And he's certainly had an influence on the 21st century by people who don't even know Hemingway's work, but they're getting it through other people. I'd say Dashiell Hammett, Raymond Chandler, and James Cain are some others.

Do you have a favorite Elmore Leonard novel? Is there one that stands out for you?

JRL: *Hombre*. I've read it several times. It's my favorite. People always ask, "What do you like better—crime, Western, horror?" I don't know. It depends. But I do think sometimes I lean towards the Western. I like the stripped down situations that Westerns allow and the lack of technological involvement and things like that. That may have something to do with it. But I think it's just such a straightforward and yet powerful tale. I like the film based on it, too. I've watched that film I don't know how many times. It's very much like the book. I think that would be my choice for the Leonard novels.

If I had to pick one after that, I'd probably pick *52 Pickup* or *City Primeval*.

You mentioned the film Hombre. *What are some of the other films you like the most that are based on Leonard's work, and what would you say are the films you like the least?*

JRL: I like *Hombre* the best. That's the one I really, really like. After that, probably *Jackie Brown*, I think. I would put that novel, *Rum Punch*, high on my list as well. I think *Jackie Brown* comes close to being a perfect film. It's my favorite Tarantino film, and I guess it's his first three or four films that I like best. That one I love, and I think it is because it's more Elmore Leonard than maybe Quentin Tarantino. Not a slug on him, but it's just to say I'm already an Elmore Leonard fan, so here's a guy who's doing it right.

I think the problem with adaptations a lot of times is [that] people feel the absolute need to change everything. And though there are certainly changes, that's pretty much the book. And you can watch it over and over, just like with *Hombre*. That's one of the reasons why I like those films—they're highly re-watchable. Some of the others, not so much.

As far as least... He was done badly several times. There was one that was filmed twice. *The Big Bounce* (1969, 2004). Not one of my favorite books of his, anyway, but I think the two film versions of it are just dreadful.

Are there any Elmore Leonard novels that don't resonate with you very much?

JRL: I like all of his novels on some level. And my least favorite Elmore Leonard is better than most people's best novel. You're judging it from a different level. There's another one called *The Hunted* (1977) that didn't hit me quite as hard. I enjoyed it, it was just less memorable for me. I like all of his books. That's one of the things I can't say about everybody. I've never read a Leonard book that I actually disliked.

Leonard wrote for decades before truly breaking out and becoming recognized at the level he is now. He had successes but didn't really explode until the eighties and then even more in the nineties. As a writer who's written for decades yourself and has slowly received more and more attention, is this an aspect of Leonard's career that is of interest to you?

JRL: I relate to it. I sure do. I don't know why that's true of his career, and my own career I honestly don't know why either. But I have to say that I've really liked it a lot being just that way because you stay new longer. You stay fresh longer because you're constantly rediscovered, you're constantly built up, you're constantly stacked up. I'm probably better known now and doing better work and getting more recognition now than when I was first making a splash in the eighties. I made a little splash then and I certainly had a following and that thing built and built. People still call me a "cult writer." I'm a big damn cult. I'm happy for that, but it's really nice in a way to just be one of those writers that keeps on coming. I love the fact that I've become a respected writer and an influential writer for some people, and someone who's even been imitated to some degree. I do see that connection, and I understand that for him it might not have been good or it may have been good. I don't know. But for me, it's been wonderful that way. I wouldn't have had it any other way.

Are there any other aspects of Elmore Leonard's career that you find inspirational or that speak to you regarding your own work or career?

JRL: I didn't know Leonard personally, although I did meet him. I was on a panel with him once in Scottsdale or Phoenix—I forget exactly where—and we were on a film panel. He said, "You're the only one up there who knows what he's talking about." I thought, "Wow! That's great! Elmore Leonard!" And I have a postcard from him somewhere. That's the extent of it. And it was complimenting my writing. He put three sentences of my story I'd written, and I thought that was great. Outside of that, I hadn't really had any contact with him.

What I always observed from the outside, and I didn't know the inside, was that he always approached what he did with class. He believed in what he did. He knew he was good. You have to know you're good. That's not the same thing as being immodest. But you don't jump out of a plane if you've never packed a parachute. That's not the way you do it. He knew he was good, and he knew he had earned his place. Those things I admired about him. But he was not immodest. He was somebody that had class. He was somebody that you aspired to be, at least in how you presented yourself to the public. I think I did learn from that. I'd like to think I was already trying to move into being that kind of person anyway, but certainly, he's a great example.

12

Peter Leonard

Born in 1951, Peter Leonard was the second of Elmore Leonard's five children (Jane, Peter, Christopher, Bill, and Katy). He has followed in his father's footsteps in multiple ways. First, like his father, he worked in advertising (for twenty-nine years). He was a founding partner at the Leonard, Mayer, and Tocco agency, which created award-winning advertising for the likes of Volkswagen of America, Audi of America, Hiram Walker, and Pennzoil. (His older sister Jane also worked there.)

But perhaps even more significantly, he later became a respected crime and mystery author like his father. He published his first book, *Quiver*, in 2008 to great acclaim. A *Guardian* review of the novel heralded his arrival: "Peter Leonard has kept his writing taut and, like his father, conveys much of the tough and uncompromising plot in dialogue. This is a very assured debut that improves as you read it, and the conclusion is terrific." As of this writing, Peter Leonard has published nine novels. In 2018, he published his eighth novel, *Raylan Goes to Detroit*, adding a fifth installment to his father's Raylan Givens series. (The four previous books were *Pronto*, 1993, *Riding the Rap*, 1995, *Fire in the Hole*, 2001, and *Raylan*, 2011.)

ANDREW J. RAUSCH: *What was it like growing up with Elmore as a father?*

PETER LEONARD: It was fun. He was a kid himself. He would play games with us, hide and seek and others. He would make up stories and read them to us before we went to bed. And they were pretty good, I have to say. He always had a BB gun and taught all the kids—there were five of us—how to shoot cans from a distance. He was an unusual father, to say the least. He was extremely funny and good natured.

I remember one time, we were in his backyard. He had a swimming pool. A bunch of us were in the water fooling around and we saw Elmore's second wife, Joan, on the roof cleaning out the gutters. My brother Bill said, "Dad, why is Joan on the roof?" And Elmore said,

"'Cause she can't write books!" He was witty that way. He was constantly coming up with really funny lines and you can see that in his work.

He also had this incredible ability to concentrate. I was seven or eight, and I remember going down to the basement. That's where Elmore worked, in this very spartan room with cinder block walls. In retrospect, it looked like a prison cell. He didn't even hear me come down the stairs, he was so lost in concentration. Across the room, there were all these yellow pieces of paper that were crumpled up around the wastebasket. Scenes that didn't make it. Shots that missed. Then Elmore would see me and I'd walk over and sit on his lap. He'd read me a scene he'd written.

And growing up, no matter where we went on vacation Elmore would write. We'd be in Florida with a group of people for Easter break, and while all the parents were sitting around the pool smoking and drinking, Elmore was a few feet off from everybody with a yellow pad and a pen in his hand, lost in thought. I remember so many examples of this.

Another time, I had a couple friends over. This was when I was in high school. We were watching a University of Michigan football game and listening to the new Jimi Hendrix album. Elmore was in the next room, about twenty feet away, writing *Valdez Is Coming* (1970). When my friends left, he said, "It was a good day. I wrote eight pages," and I said, "How could you possibly write with all the noise?" He said, "I just drown it out." That was Elmore.

When you first started writing, what kind of advice did he give you? Did you show him your early writings?

P.L.: That's a good question. I wrote stories in college. I took a couple of creative writing classes, and when I graduated I sent Elmore a short story. It was six pages long. He wrote me a three page critique, the gist of which was, "All your characters look and sound the same. They're like strips of leather dying in the sun." Which sounds weird to me today, because Elmore didn't use metaphors. It sounded like he was overwriting. So I didn't write another word of fiction for twenty-seven years. His critique wasn't the thing that discouraged me. I got on with my life. I got a job and got married. I was in the advertising business. I wrote ads. But writing a novel was always there in the back of my head.

Years later, I went to a meeting at Volkswagen, our big client, and I was presenting a new campaign. The ad manager at VW took the first storyboard, looked at it, and threw it across the conference room like a frisbee. He was doing it in fun. He wasn't mad at us. But it was frustrating just the same. I stopped at Elmore's on the way home. I was wearing a sport coat and a tie, and he was wearing Levi's and a Nine Inch Nails t-shirt. He had a bounce in his step and a Virginia Slims 100 in his hand. He picked up a piece of paper and he said, "This is a scene from *The Hot Kid* (2001) I wrote today."

That was my epiphany. On the way home I thought, if I'm ever going to write a novel, I'd better get to it. Six months later, I started writing *Quiver*. I sat in the living room. Two of my kids were doing their homework while I was writing longhand on a yellow legal pad. A year later, I had a book. I ended up sending it to Elmore's agent, Andrew Wylie. One of his guys, Jeff Posternak, read it, liked it, and passed it around. I guess the opinion was unanimous and they took me on. It was a great thing.

What was Elmore's reaction when you sold your first novel?

P.L.: He was thrilled. He thought it was fantastic. I remember I was invited to a Borders bookstore to give a talk and do a signing, and I said, "Elmore, I'm really nervous!" He said, "You're nervous? They're coming to see you! Why would you be nervous?" That advice really helped me. It got me through the first signing without any problem, and then all the signings since then.

How much additional pressure is put on a novelist when you're the son of a literary icon? I would assume that adds more pressure.

P.L.: Oh my god, yes. Elmore cast a long shadow and as he got more and more famous, everything I wrote was compared to him. Fair or not, that's the way it was. Sometimes the reviews were scathing and sometimes they were very complimentary. When I got a really good review, I'd call Elmore and read it to him. A couple said, "Peter Leonard is as good as his dad! He's the same kind of stuff, the tradition. Young Leonard is on his way!" That kind of stuff. I'd read that to Elmore and he liked it.

Did you two ever talk about literary critics? What did he think about them?

P.L.: He thought that most of them didn't know what they were talking about. They were showing off and they were writing instead of just telling about his story; they were trying to embellish their own style. He just didn't buy it. He didn't care for critics or anyone messing with his work, including editors. He got to the point where he was so famous that no editors wanted to mess with him, and that's the way he liked it.

Are there any conversations with him regarding writing that really stand out in your mind?

P.L.: Elmore would talk about how to start a book. He said, "You've gotta grab the reader immediately and not let go." So I said, "Like what?" He took out *Unknown Man No. 89* (1977) and read me the first paragraph. It says, "A friend of Ryan said to him one time, 'Yeah, but at least you don't take any shit from anybody.' Ryan said to his friend, 'I don't know. The way things have been going, maybe it's about time I started taking some.' Ryan's sister drove him down to the Detroit police car auction, where he bought a 1970 maroon and white Cougar for $270. His sister didn't like the Cougar because it had four bullet holes in the door, on the driver's side. Ryan said he didn't mind the holes. Didn't mind? He loved them." That's a good way to get a reader interested pretty quickly.

For those of us who never met Elmore in person, draw us a picture of him. What was he like as a person?

P.L.: He was an intelligent, interested, down to earth, funny person. He would talk to anyone. He wasn't full of himself. He didn't think a lot of himself. He would tell me about conversations he had with the mailman. We used to play tennis at a public court and people would say things to him and he was always polite. We'd be out to dinner and someone would say, "Oh, Mr. Leonard, I love your book." And he'd say thanks and then they would talk for a few minutes. He was that kind of guy. Approachable. Reachable. He was mature, and yet he was silly too. He was a good guy who was also a product of the Depression, so money was always a concern of his, and making sure he had enough because when he was a little kid, a lot of people didn't. But he would also give money to all kinds of organizations. Pretty much anybody that asked. He would loan money to friends. He was very generous.

That's Elmore Leonard.

You mentioned earlier there was a time when Elmore was wearing a Nine Inch Nails shirt. Was he a rock fan? Was he still rocking out at seventy?

P.L.: Yes, he was. Joe Cocker was his favorite. *Mad Dogs & Englishmen* (album, 1970). We went to see him in concert. Elmore loved the show.

One day my father ran into Steven Tyler on the street in Birmingham, our hometown. They started talking and he invited Steven and the band to come to his house. They stopped over on a Sunday afternoon. I wasn't there, but most of my brothers and sisters were. They had a blast with Aerosmith! Swimming, playing tennis, and listening to stories. Elmore loved Steven because Steven would tell him things—inside stuff about what goes on in a band.

Did Elmore talk much about his screenwriting? Was that something he enjoyed?

P.L.: He really disliked screenwriting. Part of it was adapting his own book. He already knew what was going to happen, so he found that boring. He said dealing with Hollywood was really difficult. Nobody told the truth and none of the screenwriters knew how to write. Everything was negative in his experience.

Much has been made of Elmore being the Dickens of Detroit. He lived there and frequently wrote novels that took place there. In real life, did Elmore have a genuine affinity for the city, or did he just write about Detroit because it was a location he knew well?

P.L.: He loved the city. I remember him taking my brothers and I downtown for lunch and dinner. One day, he took us to a restaurant and told us the facts of life, which is kind of funny, in retrospect. We were so young we didn't want to hear about it. It was too much. [Laughs.]

How old were you?

P.L.: I was probably ten. My brothers were seven and six. We didn't know what was going on.

Elmore was not a criminal, a street thug, or a cowboy. Beyond those obvious things, do you see any similarities between him and the characters he wrote?

P.L.: Not really. He couldn't ride a horse and I don't think he ever robbed a bank or a liquor store. But he knew how to develop characters that did. He had the right sound and attitude to make them talk and bring them to life. And he liked his bad guys way more than his good guys. I asked him why and he said, "They're more interesting. More fun."

He wrote a lot of Westerns but lived in Detroit. Having not spent much time in that type of atmosphere, what drew him to that genre? Did he talk about that with you?

P.L.: When he started writing Westerns were extremely popular.

Perspectives on Elmore Leonard

There were tons of movies and TV shows. Elmore didn't know anything about the West, so he subscribed to *Arizona Highways* magazine. That's where he'd get the descriptions of the different kinds of plants, mountains, and desert scenery. That's how he did it. And then Westerns dried up, so he turned to crime fiction. In a way, his modern day heroes and villains are not unlike his heroes and villains in the old west. Raylan Givens is a great example. Quick story regarding *Raylan*: Elmore was at a book sellers convention in Texas in the early nineties. A guy came up to him and said, "Mr. Leonard, I love your work. My name's Raylan Givens." Elmore looked at him and said, "I love your name." Then he thought to himself, "This is a book!" Elmore told me it was one of the best names he'd ever heard.

Chili Palmer's name came from a real person as well.

P.L.: Exactly. Chili was a private investigator in Miami. Elmore loved the name. Chili was a good guy at first but then he wanted money. I think Elmore got the studio to pay him based on the success of *Get Shorty* (1995). And Elmore gave him some money too.

Elmore loved names. Chili and Raylan. A guy named Juicy Mouth, from *Freaky Deaky* (1988). Mel Bandy and Teddy Cass from *The Hunted* (1977). Harry Arno from *Pronto (1993)*. Miley Mitchell, who was a friend of my sister, Jane, was the name of a hooker in *The Moonshine War* (1970). I said to Elmore, "How did Miley's parents feel about that?" He said, "I don't think they read the book."

Around the time Glitz *was published, some publications called your father an "overnight sensation," which is funny because he had been writing for over thirty years. Did he ever talk about that?*

P.L.: Yes. He said, "I'm an overnight sensation after writing twenty-three books!" He thought it was funny, but it also galled him a bit that it took him so long to get there. Elmore and I would talk about the names on the best-seller list, and he would say routinely, "Nobody on the list knows how to write." And then later on, when he was on it, I said, "Yeah, but you're on the list." And he said, "That's different."

Elmore had a second, even bigger breakthrough after the release of the film adaptation of Get Shorty *(1990) and all of a sudden, he was the hottest writer around. What was that newfound stardom like for Elmore? Did it change him in any way?*

P.L.: No, he didn't change at all, but he loved the notoriety. He loved the fact that he had been discovered and had achieved this success with a movie that made money. That really did catapult him into a different league. As a result of that, Tarantino did *Jackie Brown* (1997) and then *Out of Sight* (1998) was made. He was making a lot of money and his books were doing well. I think that was the pinnacle of his writing career.

Tarantino talks about when he was a kid, he got caught stealing a copy of The Switch *(1978) from K-Mart and got arrested. Then he claims he went back and stole it. He had always been a fan of Elmore's work. What did Elmore think of Quentin, and did they hit it off?*

P.L.: Elmore liked Quentin and he liked his movies. Tarantino adapted the book *Rum Punch* (1992). He changed the title, the name of the main character and wrote a script that was one hundred and sixty-two pages, which is really long for a film. He called my father up and said, "Elmore, I hope you're not mad. Here's what I've done." And Elmore said, "Just make a good movie." Quentin did and everyone was happy.

Let's talk about Justified *for a moment. I got the feeling Elmore was very proud of* Justified.

P.L.: He loved it! He thought the writers got his sound, his voice and were able to interpret his writing. Graham Yost, the showrunner, had rubber bracelets made for everybody involved in the series. Each one had the initials "WWED?," which meant "What Would Elmore Do?" Graham put together a team of writers that really knew what they were doing. The fact that they did six seasons of *Justified* based on a short story is really kind of amazing.

What do you remember about the day Elmore passed away?

P.L.: He was divorced from his third wife and he was dating a girl who was fifty-eight, and he was eighty-seven. She had moved into his house that afternoon. She called me early that evening and said, "I think your dad just had a stroke!" She was a former nurse. I raced over. I lived only half a mile from my father, so I got there very quickly, followed by EMS. Sure enough, he had had a stroke. We went to the hospital and he went to ICU. My sisters arrived just after me. It was sad. It was tough. It was emotional. Elmore was in the hospital for a week. Then the family decided to bring him home. We had a bed set up in his writing room, which was also the living room. He died the next morning. We knew it was going to happen, but it was still a shocker.

Perspectives on Elmore Leonard

The funeral was a major event, attended by actors, producers, agents, friends and family—with a reception in Elmore's enormous backyard.

Your father always expressed in public that he wasn't concerned with his legacy. Behind closed doors, do you believe that was true?

P.L.: I think so. I think he knew he'd done as good a job as he could do and had become famous. He loved receiving the National Book Award for Lifetime Achievement in 2012. Martin Amis introduced him. I actually have part of his speech right here. He wrote something that was so great. Let me read it. Martin said, "The essence of Mr. Leonard is to be found in the use of the present participle. What this means in effect is that he's discovered a way of slowing down and suspending the English sentence—or let's say the American sentence, because Mr. Leonard is as American as jazz. Instead of writing 'Warren Ganz lived up in Manalpan,' he writes: 'Warren Ganz, living up in Manalpan'; he writes, 'Bobby saying' and then opens up the quotes. He writes, 'Dawn saying.' We're not in the imperfect sense ('Dawn was saying') or the present tense ('Dawn says') or the historic present, 'Dawn said.' We're in a kind of marijuana tense; 'Dawn saying,' creamy, wandering, weak-verbed. Such sentences seem to open up a lag in time through which Mr. Leonard easily slides, gaining entry into his players' minds. He doesn't just show you what these people say and do, he shows you how they breathe." How do you top that?

What was Elmore working on at the time of his death?

P.L.: He was writing a book called *Blue Dreams*. He had probably written a hundred pages. At the funeral, people came up to me and said, are you going to finish your dad's novel? Something that had never occurred to me. As I thought about it, I decided that it was just not a good idea. There's something sacred about that unfinished prose. I didn't want to do anything to tarnish it or step on it. My brother, Chris, some days later said, "Why don't you write a *Raylan* novel?" And I thought, that is a good idea. The *Justified* writing team had set a precedent. I thought, why don't I take a shot at it? So that's how that came about.

I think placing the story in Detroit was brilliant, considering so many of Elmore's stories took place in Detroit. Do you want to talk about that?

P.L.: At the time, Raylan was in Harlan County, Kentucky. That had been done. In previous books, he'd been in Miami, and he'd been in Rapallo, Italy, so I thought, we'll just bring him to Detroit, the city I know. I had spent a month riding with the U.S. Marshals in Detroit, San Diego, and El Centro, California. I had a lot of great material and knew a lot about how the marshals operate—how they arrest fugitives, and the other things that they do. I thought, this is perfect. I'll have Raylan come to Detroit and we'll put him on the fugitive task force! And that's exactly what happened.

Were you at all intimidated by continuing Raylan's journey?

P.L.: Not at all. I had read all the books that Raylan appeared in. I watched much of the TV series. Raylan was so familiar to me that I felt at ease jumping into his boots and putting his Stetson on. I felt that I could do this. The reviews have been pretty favorable.

In writing the book, did that make you feel somewhat more connected or closer to Elmore in his absence?

P.L.: I didn't think of it that way. I spent so much time with Elmore that I felt close to him because we talked so much. We traveled. One day, Elmore's third wife came home and said to him, "All right, that's it, I'm not making dinner for you anymore. I don't have time." So Elmore started coming to my house for dinner, which was really fun. He would pull up in his 1996 Volkswagen Cabriolet, get out of the car, come in and put a bottle of wine on the counter in the kitchen. He'd do a little tap dance and light a Virginia Slims 100 and start talking about writing. Typically starting with what he'd written that day and then writing in general. It was really fun. Every night was fun. He'd just throw out these little gems. These nuggets of wisdom.

Now that you've written Raylan Goes to Detroit, *will you be writing any more of these books?*

P.L.: I think *Raylan Goes to Detroit* is my one and only Raylan book. I've already written another novel, *Sweet Dreams,* and the main character is the lone female on the fugitive task force in Detroit. I spent time with this girl whose nickname is Sully. I got to know her very well, rode around with her for a couple days while she was arresting fugitives. We just talked about all kinds of things—movies, books, recipes, whatever. It was interesting to see how she reacted to all of the alpha-males on the task force. She held her own. She was a markswoman and knew what she was doing. There was so much contrast there that I decided I had to write a book starring her as the main character.

When Elmore found out I had a female lead in my first novel, he said, "How's that going?" I said, "How do you write a female main character?" He said, "You picture a girl you went to high school with that had seven brothers. She knows how to throw a curveball. She's tough." I thought, wow! That's it!

I've got a photo of Elmore on the wall in my office and it's like he's looking over my shoulder. If I make a mistake, I can hear him saying, "If it sounds like writing, rewrite it."

13

Charles Matthau

The son of actor Walter Matthau and actress Carol Grace (and also the godson of Charlie Chaplin), Charles "Charlie" Matthau grew up in the film industry. As a young boy he appeared in several of his father's films including *Charley Varrick* (1973), *Bad News Bears* (1976), and *House Calls* (1978). He then went to work for his father's production company, Walcar Productions.

Matthau then set his sights on directing. He made his directorial debut with the Cannon Films comedy *Doin' Time on Planet Earth* (1988). He then directed his father and Ellen Burstyn in the 1991 telefilm *Mrs. Lambert Remembers Love*. In 1995 he reunited his father and his frequent co-star Jack Lemon in an adaptation of Truman Capote's *The Grass Harp* (1951). Matthau would direct one more film featuring his iconic father (*The Marriage Fool*, 1998) before the elder Matthau's death in 2000. Matthau next directed the comedy film *Her Minor Thing* (2005) and the musical drama *Baby-O* (2009).

After that, Matthau decided to adapt Elmore Leonard's 1988 crime novel *Freaky Deaky*. Matthau adapted the screenplay himself (his first screenwriting credit) and cast Billy Burke, Christian Slater, Crispin Glover, Michael Jai White, Andy Dick, Gloria Hendry, and Bill Duke.

ANDREW J. RAUSCH: *When did you first become aware of Elmore Leonard?*

CHARLES MATTHAU: I'm not sure. I've always been kind of a voracious reader, so it was probably pretty early on. I love crime stories.

Are there any of his novels that you really enjoy (besides Freaky Deaky*)?*

CM: Yeah, several. I've read several of them and I always love anything he writes.

What stands out the most to you about Elmore Leonard's writing?

CM: I think just that he makes it look so easy. Most people would say the dialogue. And the dialogue is great, but he's got a brilliant mind and a brilliant sense of humor. He has a very ironic look at life. He's just a pleasure to read. I also appreciate his economy of words. I'm sure you're familiar with his rules of writing, where he says cut out the boring parts and use as few words as possible. I appreciate that Hemingway-esque style, having read too many books that err in the opposite direction.

How did you come to option the rights to Freaky Deaky?

CM: I was working on a movie that was filming in Michigan called *An Ordinary Killer* (2003). One of my coworkers asked, "Do you want to have dinner with my friend Elmore?" So of course I jumped at the chance and went to this dinner, and I asked Elmore if there were any of his books that he really liked that weren't made into movies yet. He mentioned *Freaky Deaky*, which I had not yet read. After I read it, he was kind enough to let me option it. It took me about a year to write the script. He would give me notes on it and was very helpful and supportive with that process.

You adapted the novel yourself. If I'm not mistaken, that's your only screenplay credit.

CM: I think that's probably right. I've worked on the scripts for most of the movies that I directed, but mainly polishing, as directors sometimes do. But in this case, I was the only screenwriter.

What made you decide to tackle this one on your own?

CM: Well, I thought I had a pretty good take on it. In retrospect, I am not so sure that *Freaky Deaky* is one of the more natural titles to be a movie that Elmore has written. I say that because the plot—the bare bones element of the plot—is kind of silly. Consequently, since it's not really going to work as a thriller, as some of Elmore's books would work, this was more of a comedy. I think that if I had to do it over again, I would prefer something that had a more exciting plot that I could then add some humor to. I notice when people see the movie now, people who are expecting some kind of great, gripping crime story are disappointed. And people who go in there not really knowing that much about Elmore, but just hoping for a fun, silly movie, tend to like the movie better. It's not a movie that is really going to appeal to hardcore Elmore fans, and I totally get why.

What can you tell me about the process of adapting the novel? What was your process? Did you know upfront what you were going to do? Did it evolve through multiple drafts?

CM: Yeah, there were multiple drafts. The time period got changed.

With a movie like this, where the plot is not necessarily going to keep you at the edge of your chair, it's important to find an actor or actors that you really enjoy being around. I talked to John Travolta about playing Chris, and he wanted to do it, but we didn't have enough money. Our budget couldn't afford him. It would've been a different kind of movie, I think, if we had had him because he's one of those actors where you almost could just watch him in anything and fall in love. The plot doesn't even matter. I saw him in this steamboat racing movie that he just did, and it's not *Citizen Kane* (1941), but he is so enjoyable and so watchable, he could sit there and read the phone book and I would love it. I think actors like that are hard to get. I think my father was like that. There are some of my father's movies that, plot-wise, wouldn't really go anywhere, but you'd enjoy it because it was him.

Did knowing that this was Elmore's favorite novel add extra pressure when you were making the film?

CM: Well, he kept changing what was his favorite! [Laughs] He told me this was his favorite that hadn't been made yet, and I saw in an interview where he said *Freaky Deaky* was his favorite. But then I saw interviews with him where he said others were his favorite too. I suppose it's a bit more pressure because I admired Elmore so much, but again, what makes a great novel or someone's favorite novel does not necessarily lend itself to a film. I think the book is better than the film, as is often the case.

When you met him, what was he like in person?

CM: He couldn't have been nicer. Just unassuming, complete gentleman. I showed him the movie and he was very nice about it and found a lot of things to praise about it, even though I think he was probably ultimately underwhelmed with the movie. He found several things he liked about it, which I appreciated.

I don't think he liked very many of his movies, honestly.

CM: Wasn't it *The Big Bounce* (1969) that he said was the worst movie he ever saw? And then they remade it (2004) and he said *that* was the worst movie he'd ever seen.

I was glad to see that you kept Freaky Deaky *in Detroit and actually filmed it there. A lot of the adaptations have changed the locations. Did you feel that it was important to keep the story in Detroit?*

CM: Yes, I did.

When we spoke previously you told me there was some sort of program through the state of Michigan that helped you make the film. Could you tell me about that?

CM: There was a tax credit program in Michigan. That was both a blessing and a curse because it led to the movie being financed, because the family that financed the movie owned a lot of real estate in Michigan. They were able to finance the tax credit against their status of income and do well with that. But it also had to be filmed in Michigan and the unions are very strong there. On *Freaky Deaky*, which had a budget of six million dollars, we spent $900,000 on transportation. And one third of the movie takes place in one location. So we actually ended up spending more on transportation than on cast. It was a mixed blessing, but it was certainly the right place to film *Freaky Deaky*, storywise.

I recall that there were other actors who sort of came and went, besides John Travolta.

CM: Yes. At one point, when it became apparent that having John in the movie was not going to work out, which broke my heart, Matt Dillon was going to play Chris. Then William H. Macy was going to play Woody. Then I think William H. Macy had to go back to *Shameless*, so we weren't able to get started in time. So we missed out on him. I was able to replace him with my childhood friend, Crispin Glover, who I think did a wonderful job. Matt changed his mind at the last minute and decided not to do it, which I understand he does a lot. I guess he's notorious for getting cold feet at the last minute. We lost him about a week before we had to start shooting. So I was able to replace him with Billy Burke, who was an actor that I had worked with before on a musical that I directed called *Baby-O*. He agreed to sub at the last minute and forty-eight hours later he was shooting.

We also had Sienna Miller playing the role of Greta, and I still don't know what happened with that. Apparently, one of the producers at the time called her agent, and I had met with her and she was all ready to do it, and then her agent said that she wasn't available during that time period. Again, we were kind of locked in to filming at this time period. Then we cast someone else. Then, once we were in production, I got a call from her manager saying, "Well, I thought Sienna was going to do that part?" And I said, "Well, I thought so too. We wanted her, but she was not available." The manager said, "Your producer should've called me instead of calling the agent." And then the agent, I think, blamed his assistant. It was a just big cluster fuck. But I was really sorry about that as well, because it would've been wonderful to get to work with Sienna Miller.

You mentioned Crispin Glover. Both Crispin Glover and Andy Dick have a reputation for being a bit eccentric at times. What were those guys like to work with on the film?

CM: Crispin was great. I've known him since we both went to the Merman School for Gifted Children in Bel-Air. I've known him my whole life. I get his process. He's very intellectual and cerebral and brilliant. He thinks about things to death. I get that because I can also be that way sometimes, although without maybe the brilliant part. [Laughs] I can definitely get lost in my head. So I had a delightful experience with him.

And Andy Dick?

CM: He was fine.

Michael Jai White really seemed to connect with his character, Donnell. What do you remember about working with Michael?

CM: He was very professional. The one story I remember about him is when he throws the dynamite into the pool. The pool was located very far away, so I was going to do two cuts, one where he throws the dynamite and then one from the other direction where it lands in the pool. He goes, "Oh, I can throw it in there from here." And I said, "Yeah, but I want it to go from the center of the pool." And he goes, "No problem!" It was *really* far away. So just to humor him I said, "Okay, sure. Let's try." So we set up a shot where the camera follows the dynamite into the pool out of his hand. I thought there was no way he was gonna make it. On the first take, he threw it like an Olympic athlete and it landed exactly in the middle of the pool. I couldn't believe it. I say, "Well that was just amazing." He was getting cocky [laughs] and was like, "You want me to do it again?" And I laughed because I thought he was kidding. Then we did another take just because I wanted to see if he could do it again. And he did it again. He's amazing.

Gloria Hendry and Bill Duke are both legends. How did they come to the film and what were they like?

CM: They were awesome. Couldn't have been sweeter, couldn't have been nicer. I remember thinking about Bill Duke when I was actually reading the novel. I always wanted him to play that part, and he was nice enough to do it. And Gloria was sort of an idea I got later on, and she was a delight.

How about Christian Slater? How did he come to the project?

CM: Christian came to the project, again, it was sort of a ... once Matt fell out of the project at the last minute, it was sort a cascade effect. We had to replace four of the top six roles with less than a week to go. We got lucky with the way it turned out, especially considering what happened. I had worked with Christian's mother on *The Grass Harp*. She was a casting director. I always liked his work very much and had met him before, but we had never worked together. And he came in at the last minute, and I thought he was a terrific Skip.

When you first read the novel, what were you thinking when you read the scene the movie starts with, where the guy's sitting on the bomb and Billy Burke and the other cop walk outside and let him blow up? It just seems so cinematic on the page.

CM: It reminded me of the scene from *Lethal Weapon 2 (1989)* where they had a similar scene. But they actually stole that from Elmore, because he had written *Freaky Deaky* before that. What I liked so much about *Get Shorty* (1995), other than the fact that John Travolta was in it is the fact that they didn't try to be funny and that they played every-thing straight. They didn't have reaction shots, which I know Elmore hates and so do I, of actors laughing at the other actor saying a line, because it takes you out of a movie. But the thing about *Freaky Deaky* is it mainly depends on the comedy to work. It's hard to sustain for ninety minutes when what's on the page is more smiles than laugh-out-loud funny. I think if you're sort of just going into it, not necessarily from the perspective of "this is from the guy that wrote *Hombre* (1961) and *52 Pick-Up* (1986) and *Get Shorty*" and you just find it on Netflix or something and look at it as a "popcorn" film, people enjoy it more than Elmore Leonard aficionados who come to the film with a certain type of thing in mind.

You placed marquee signs advertising your father's films, The Front Page *(1974) and* The Taking of Pelham One Two Three *(1974), in the film. What made you decide to do that?*

CM: We had to use something, so I thought why not pay homage to the Great One. He had made those two films in that year and it was coming during a period where he would go from playing Willy Clark in *The Sunshine Boys* (1975) to playing an action hero in *The Laughing Policeman* or *The Taking of Pelham One Two Three* or *Charley Varrick*. He was so versatile.

You went through all of these crazy things and you were trying to get the movie done on schedule. You had people coming and going. At the end of the day, what aspects of Freaky Deaky *are you the most proud of?*

CM: I think it's a fun film if you like silly. It's certainly not the best Elmore film by a long shot. It is not *Hombre* or John Travolta, Gene Hackman, and Danny DeVito in *Get Shorty*.

Overall, was the experience of working on the film a positive one for you?

CM: It was positive. I had a great time, learned a lot, worked with nice people, and we made a fun little film. I'm happy with the way it came out, if you judge the movie on its own merits as opposed to part of the Elmore Leonard canon. I feel very blessed and very grateful to have gotten to meet Elmore and work with him and become friends with him. The overall experience of making the film was a good one.

14

Charles J. Rzepka

Boston University English professor Charles J. Rzepka is the foremost academic expert on the writings of Elmore Leonard. Rzepka, who earned his Ph.D. at Berkeley and was Boston University's 2006 Scholar/ Teacher of the Year, first wrote about Leonard in the *Companion to Crime Fiction* (2010), a volume he co-edited with Lee Horsley. Prior to this, Rzepka had written essays on writers as varied as Anton Chekhov, John Keats, and Raymond Chandler, but he found Leonard's work particularly interesting. He soon set to writing a full-length study for which he interviewed the author several times. (The interviews themselves are collected in their entirety on the CrimeCulture website: https://www.crimeculture. com/?page_id=3435.) The resulting book, *Being Cool: The Work of Elmore Leonard*, was published by Johns Hopkins University Press in 2013 to great acclaim. The book was a Macavity Award finalist and received top honors from the House of Crime and Mystery's Reader's Choice awards and Killer Nashville's Silver Falchion awards. The book is now available in paperback.

In addition, Rzepka has chaired a special session on Leonard's work, "Elmore Leonard: Kids, Killers, Comedy," at the 2016 conference of the Modern Language Association of America, and lectured on the topics "Elmore Leonard and Hemingway: The Lessons of Free Indirect Discourse" (2012) and "*Criminis Virumque Cano*: Civilian Warcraft in Elmore Leonard's Crime Fiction" (2013) at symposia hosted by the American Literary Association. He wrote "Bouncing Big: Elmore Leonard's Primal Scene" for *Clues: A Journal of Detection* in 2015. He recently edited *Critical Essays on Elmore Leonard: If It Sounds Like Writing* (Wiley, 2020), an anthology to which he also contributed one essay, "'It's the way they're done': Style and Legerdemain in *Out of Sight*," and co-wrote a second, "Disjointed *Djibouti*: Elmore Leonard's Final Metafiction," with George Grella.

ANDREW J. RAUSCH: *Swag (1976) was the first Elmore Leonard book you read. Did you recognize how different and important his work was immediately, or was that something you gradually came to recognize?*

14. Charles J. Rzepka

CHARLES J. RZEPKA: No, I don't think I did at first. I just really enjoyed it and thought I had to read more. I think somebody said, "Oh, you're from Detroit? Have you read Elmore Leonard?" and they recommended this book. And I was hooked. It was only after reading more of his books that I realized he might be worth taking seriously as a writer, and I taught detective fiction and crime fiction so I saw the virtues in what he was doing. One thing led to another, and when I agreed to co-edit *Companion to Crime Fiction* it seemed like there was an obvious niche for an essay on Elmore Leonard there. He was quite a big presence on the crime writing scene at that time, certainly since the seventies, and then up to his death. I'm not sure if he's maintained that level of popularity since then. I don't know what the current sales figures are.

What aspect of his work speaks to you personally?

CJR: It's hard to choose one thing off the top of my head. The Detroit locales, obviously. Stylistically, I think it's the effortless way that his plots eventuate in some of the most improbable coincidences that you can imagine—and *beyond* what you can imagine—and still seem believable. You have to stand back and really look at or think about it to realize how improbable some of them are. That's because he sets them up in such a way that they are the result of dozens and dozens of individual, independent character decisions, and he carefully charts them. He'll have a character who ordinarily wouldn't think of doing a certain thing, who for some reason, given a particular set of circumstances, does the thing they wouldn't do, and that has repercussions. It's sort of like the butterfly flapping its wings in China causing the hurricane in Bermuda. He's really, really good at this, and I think it's because, as he said often enough, about halfway through the book he knows which character or characters to trust. And those characters carry the lead. They take over the plot and he doesn't have to contrive these improbable encounters—they contrive themselves. They seem to come about as a natural result of many deliberate but unpredictable individual decisions.

Some authors try, but just aren't good at this. [Charles] Dickens isn't good at this. In fact, Dickens is an excellent counterpoint to what Leonard does because Leonard does this so much better. With Dickens, the coincidence arrives out of the blue at the end of his plots, and some of them are simply outrageous. Like the end of *Great Expectations*, where the heroine and the hero just happen to meet at the old brewery where they first met, on this one day, this one night, at this one moment of

133

the night, after all the years that they've been separated. It seems emotionally inevitable, but it's realistically outrageous. But you never have that feeling when you're reading Leonard. And by the way, that's not the ending that Dickens originally wrote. The original ending was much more haphazard, and thus believable, where the two characters encounter each other on a crowded London street. The odds are great that they would at some time or other over the course of their lives. And, just as believably, nothing comes of it. They go their separate ways.

Some people have said that Leonard's plots are simple, but I think that's deceptive. They appear simplistic. They usually have a simple logline by which they can be described but are actually fairly complicated.

CJR: They get complicated, but not complex. By that, I mean there might be several threads going at once, but you can follow them all. You never get confused. Except perhaps in *Djibouti* (2010). There are a lot of pitfalls for the unwary reader in *Djibouti*, but that's because Leonard's deliberately playing around with jump cuts in chronology and time. It's really easy to lose your way. I had to read that book two or three times to really figure out what was happening, when was it happening ... the chronology of events. Other than that, most of the books are, as I said, complicated in that you have several threads going, but you're never confused about which one you're following or how they interact with each other.

Let's talk about Leonard's sense of place. His early crime novels almost all take place in Detroit. Then a lot of the later ones take place in Florida. I think the Detroit novels have a grittier feel than the later novels. Do you think that is a reflection on the locale, or do you think that's just his writing at the time? I think his style became a little slicker and more polished in the eighties and nineties.

CJR: I'm not sure that the style changes much due to locale. I guess it depends on how you define style. Detroit just is grittier than Miami. It's grimmer. At the time he turned away from westerns to start writing about crime, Detroit was beginning its long slide into eventual bankruptcy a couple of decades later.

Places like Florida, it's sunny and happy. In Florida *noir*, the shadows are hard to see. You have to look around and pick up the rocks. In Detroit, it was always right there in front of you, at least since the riots of '67, which is about when Leonard first turned to crime writing.

There is a continuity between the earlier books—the Detroit books of the '70s—and everything he did later. I think it's that he has a persistent, over the course of his career perhaps even increasing, sense of the history of the place that he's writing about, history that's been lost. You see this in the Florida books, as well as in the Detroit books. In *52 Pickup* (1974), Bobby Shy hijacks the tourist bus. And while he and his partner are emptying the tourists' pockets, he gives them an impromptu tour of the bombed out neighborhood that was destroyed during the '67 riots and still hadn't been rebuilt by the time that book went to press.

And there's a sense of nostalgia. In *Swag*, the downtown Hudson's department store is a really big player. It's where the central heist occurs. Then just a few years later, the real Hudson store closes. Dayton-Hudson closes it down because it's not doing enough business due to white flight from the inner city. I think already, when Leonard's writing that book, he's aware of what's coming for stores like Hudson's.

Then you turn to a Florida book like *LaBrava* (1983), there's all this stuff about the older, pre-war modernist styles of hotels on South Beach. Franny Kaufman takes color photographs of them. I think Maurice Zola, he goes on and on about the now vanished Key West Railroad. It's almost as though Leonard wants to remind us of what's been lost or in jeopardy of being lost. Those hotels are in danger of being torn down and replaced with these faceless contemporary buildings that have no personality. Also, in *Glitz* (1985), there's Atlantic City, what it once was, and what it is now, after casino-blight has taken over. He's very aware of that.

There is a thread of continuity here in the sense of place. Leonard, when he writes about a place, is always aware of its history, and he is especially aware of the history that has been lost or is in jeopardy of being lost.

If I may, I'd like to add a plug here for David Geherin's book, *Scene of the Crime: The Importance of Place in Crime and Mystery Fiction* (2008). And Geherin has an essay in a new collection of critical essays that I edited for Wiley titled *Critical Essays on Elmore Leonard: If It Sounds Like Writing* (2020). Geherin has a really good take on Leonard's sense of place.

Was the essay you wrote for Companion to Crime Fiction *your first writing on Leonard?*

CJR: Yes. The third part of that collection has essays on specific writers and filmmakers. There's an essay on [Alfred] Hitchcock, for instance. There's an essay on Sir Arthur Conan Doyle and Sherlock Holmes. My essay on Leonard is one of those.

Was that when you first reached out to him? Did you speak to him in preparing for that?

CJR: No. I had never met him at the time I wrote that essay. My interviews were after. Working on the essay is what got me interested in Leonard as an academic subject and made me want to write more about him. It also let me test some of the theories I had about his writing.

At times Leonard seemed to have a distrust of literary academia. With this in mind, I wondered if he was at all hesitant to do the interviews?

CJR: Not at all. Just the opposite. I sent him a letter through his publisher. I remember the moment when I heard back from him. He sent me a handwritten letter. He said, "It sounds interesting." I think the letter ends with something like "let's make it happen." But I don't think he said how he was going to make it happen. [Laughs.]

A few days later, I'm out shopping at a supermarket and I'm on my way in from the car to do the shopping and my phone rings and it's Elmore Leonard. He says, "Can we set up a time to arrange an interview?" I said, "Sure, I'd love to do that." There I was standing in the parking lot talking to Elmore Leonard. People are walking by with their grocery carts and I think it looks like it's about to rain, but I'm not going to move. So that was how we arranged the first interview. I asked if it was okay if we did it in person, and he said, "Sure, that's fine."

I flew out to Detroit, and I remember being very nervous about whether my digital recorder was going to work. I tested it several times. I got to his neighborhood half an hour early and went to a Starbucks. I reviewed all of my notes and tested the digital recorder again. But I had no reason to be nervous. I'm sure you've heard from everyone what an affable, friendly, welcoming, courteous, and just-plain-folks kind of guy he was. And he was. He was kind, generous, and if he was interested at all in what you were doing he made as much time as you wanted or needed. I think I had close to a dozen interviews with him, and I never felt pressured to leave or that he was looking at his watch. He seemed as interested as I was in what we were saying. And if he wasn't, that just speaks to the incredible level of courtesy that he was naturally inclined to.

I'd like to add something: I think his reputed anti-intellectualism was something of a pose. I think what he hated was phonies. He hated jargon for its own sake. Jargon just means specialized talk. If you go to an auto mechanic and they start explaining what's wrong with your car and they're using words like carburetor and manifold, that's jargon. That's auto repair jargon. It's fine at the gas station, but out of place at a garden party, because it closes people out of the conversation. I think, outside the academy, coming from pointy-headed intellectuals (according to a certain stereotype), their specialized talk sounds pretentious.

Again, going back to *LaBrava*, there are some really intelligent things LaBrava, the protagonist, has to say about the art of photography and Walker Evans. It's in the context of his making fun of what a critic says about his photography—meaning to praise it—that comes right out of a *Village Voice* article that Leonard liked to cite as an example of this kind of pretentiousness. But here he was, giving me, a college professor, upwards of thirteen or fourteen hours of his time for a book that the college professor is writing about his writing. If he had the level of contempt for intellectuals that he's reputed to have had, I don't know why he'd ever have let me cross the threshold.

Leonard cultivated an image of his being an unsophisticated blue-collar guy. That's not exactly the truth. He was a very intelligent, very educated man, who seemed fairly enlightened. Why do you think he felt the need to present himself as an unsophisticated man?

CJR: He was a genuine human being, but he was also a genuine writer. By that, I mean a working writer. Part of his tool kit as a working writer was understanding his readership, and how they imagined him. I'm not saying this was insincere at all. I think he really felt this way. In lectures, public talks, interviews, he indicated his wariness of reading too much into his books and said he was just a lunch bucket guy going about his business, punching the clock. But a part of his business was maintaining that kind of persona. I think that was part of it. I don't think he went out of his way to cultivate it; it was just easy for him to fall into it because I think that he genuinely felt that he was that kind of writer.

In person, you didn't have to talk to him very long to see that he was really intelligent, and knowledgeable. One of the questions you asked me previously was "what was one of the things that most surprised you about him when you interviewed him?" I think it was when he burst out with a recitation of the *Apostles' Creed* in Greek. Sure, it was a holdover from when he was at U of D high school, being taught by Jesuits, but my god, he studied Greek! He could read it! He said he hadn't read Aristotle in Greek, but he mentioned someone else, another Greek philosopher, that he had read.

I think he was a complex individual, and the idea that he was a blue-collar Joe was important to his identity as a writer. But I also think that, for him as a person, it wasn't.

You mentioned him having an awareness of his readership. He talked about how he didn't have a real affinity for Westerns but he wrote them because that was what the market favored at the time. Then he finds the crime genre and excels at it. He wrote books that were outside the genre, such as Djibouti *or* Touch *(1987), that didn't perform as well. Do you get a sense that he wanted to write other things but felt limited by what he believed his audience expected?*

CJR: Perhaps, but in a special way. I think he wrote what he wanted to write. If he wanted to write something different or try something different, he tried something different, but he'd wait until he could afford to—in the literal sense. I think because he was a professional writer and he took his writing seriously as a profession—it provided his paycheck, it bought his house, supported his family—because he took his writing seriously as (the term I use in the book) a *techne*, a skill for making a living—in that sense, I think he felt he had to become successful enough first before he could take the financial risk to write a different book. You notice *Touch* doesn't appear until pretty well into his crime career. And *Djibouti* at the end. It's like he's saying, "Okay, I'm not going to be doing this much longer. If I'm gonna try this other thing, now's when I can afford to fail at it."

The last time I talked to him was when he was working on *Blue Dreams*, which was unfinished at his death. He said, "I think this is it. I don't think I'm going to be writing more after this." So *Djibouti*, his most experimental book, was the penultimate, the one before the last completed one, which was *Raylan*. I think he felt, "Okay, it's time for me to do this." It may have been on his mind for a while.

Touch is Leonard's version of the movie *Being There* (1979). It's that kind of book. It's got a flimflam man running a scam—nothing surprising there—and it's got a religious fanatic—a bit surprising (this is long before *Pagan Babies*)—and the young protagonist, Juvenal, the quiet, unassuming Peter Sellers character, is a devout Franciscan friar—very surprising, for a Leonard book. There's a thread of violence, but none of that is really central to Juvenal's vexed relationship to this miraculous stigmata he experiences out of the blue, the wounds of Christ appearing on his hands, feet, and side, that enables him to heal people without his even wanting to. Just by touching them or having them touch him. As a result, he gets swept up in a wave of public hysteria that almost drowns him, spiritually. It's a remarkable, remarkable book.

Do you think there is a Leonard protagonist who, more closely than the others, represents who Leonard was as a person in terms of attitude and personality?

CJR: I've mentioned *LaBrava* twice now, and Joe LaBrava is not a bad choice. He has a similar attitude towards his art, which is an outgrowth of his getting fed up with being a Secret Service agent assigned to Bess Truman's house, where there's nothing to do. He realizes he has an eye for what's going to happen next, so he becomes an excellent documentary photographer and opens a shop in South Florida. His stuff is shown in galleries nearby. He's being written about. But he has a sort of Leonardian attitude towards it all. He says, "I take pictures to make a buck." I think Leonard was very fond of that way of characterizing himself. But no one would deny that he's an artist as well.

The other thing about LaBrava that I think is rooted somewhat deeper in Leonard's personality is his attachment to those femme fatales from the B-movie era. LaBrava even says, "That's when I fell in love with these women" And that's how he leaves himself open to be exploited by Jean Shaw. So, Joe LaBrava, that's one.

Juvenal in *Touch* is another one. He's got this gift he can't control and he doesn't know what to do with. Leonard may have had that growing up—a gift for writing—and he had to wait to discover what he could do with it. And the most obvious choice, talking again about *Djibouti*, would be Dara Barr, the documentary photographer who can't decide if she wants to make a documentary to help further the work of social justice, or film a Hollywood blockbuster and get rich. Xavier, her cinematographer, is there to persuade her to take the money and run, but up to the very end, although it looks as though she's going to accept his advice, we don't know what she decides. And I love that about that book. I love that. It looks as though she's going to follow Xavier's lead, but it just never says.

I think her social conscience is very close to Leonard's. His Catholicism ran deep, although he stopped going to church during the Vatican II movement. He was influenced by the Catholic social justice movement and the Liberation Theology of the sixties and seventies. *Bandits* (1987) is a perfect example of his interest in those issues and those questions.

So those are the three characters who come to mind.

Perspectives on Elmore Leonard

As you know, both film adaptations of The Big Bounce (1969, 2004) *are pretty bad. Do you feel like there's something specific to that work that presents difficulties for adaptation?*

CJR: I do. I think that the book presents problems that can't be overcome by any film. In a lot of Hollywood adaptations of Leonard's stories, the problem is direction. What he deplored in general was directors and screenplay writers who were unable to get his sense of humor and who would wink, essentially telegraphing the humor. They'd have actors chuckling at their own jokes. They didn't get the deadpan tone of Leonard's humor. He said in one interview, "These folks don't know they're funny. Whenever you show them thinking [that] they're funny, you just stick a pin in the balloon." Or words to that effect.

I'm not sure that's so much the problem with these movies, though. I think the problem in both films is that they're dealing with a book in which the protagonist, Jack Ryan, is a loser. Just a loser. He's a loose cannon. He's a feckless, resentful kid with a chip on his shoulder. He's a 4-F Vietnam reject. He wanted more than anything to enlist and still admires the military. He has these swashbuckling fantasies about combat. Instead, he goes into Major League Baseball, as a pitcher. But he fails at the minor leagues because he can't pitch. And he ends up as a migrant worker who breaks into people's summer homes in the thumb area of Michigan.

In the first film, Ryan O'Neal is too glamorous and too sexy for this role. If I'm not mistaken they make him a Vietnam veteran. They completely turn around the premise of the book and that turns the rest of the story into nonsense. I think Jack Ryan's personality is one reason why Leonard had so much trouble selling the book. It went through 84 rejections and more before he finally managed to land it. It was originally called *Mother, This Is Jack Ryan*, which is a line he was going to give to Nancy, the *femme fatale*.

It's a line that she imagines telling her mother when she introduces her to Jack. It's a kind of slap in the face—"Mom, here's the guy I told you about, this loser, bum, petty criminal that I've hooked up with"—because she hates her mother. Her mother is this well-to-do matriarchal kind of person, and Nancy's in permanent rebellion against her. That was the original title and it just didn't work. Leonard finally went back and made major revisions to the story and it became *The Big Bounce*, which is a phrase he got from *Esquire*, from an article on "The New Woman." He was sure it was going to go viral. It was going to be the latest thing in American slang. It went nowhere so the title didn't mean anything when people read it. And the book still didn't work if you're interested in a hero because the Jack Ryan character remains anything but. He's still the loser Nancy wants to shock her mother with. He ends up in a botched burglary in which he's a party to a murder and there's broken glass all over the place from the bratty femme fatale, and he's just waiting for the cops to show up. It's a complete bust. So what's the payoff there?

I think the problem with both movie versions of this book is that they're trying to work with original material that can't be shaped into a blockbuster plot. No matter what they do with it, the odor lingers. But that's just my opinion.

Just a side note: I can understand that different times create different movie standards and production values, but the music in the first movie is so distracting! It's totally inappropriate, as I recall. It's like this bouncy, kicky finger-snapping music. It's like *77 Sunset Strip* music.

Does Elmore Leonard have a masterwork? Everyone either has a difficulty pointing to anything or, if they do, they point to a different work. Are they all masterworks? Why isn't there one particular work that resonates as the definitive masterwork?

CJR: He was the first one to say that he was basically doing the same thing over and over. He says at one point that the Jack Ryan hero is the template. (Ryan gets much more likeable, by the way.) He's basically the same hero but with different names and slightly different personalities. But they have the same basic core. I don't want to sound as though he was just cranking them out. You can group them according to different themes or aims or points of view or issues he wants to explore. You can group them by locale. But within those groups, they're adopting different perspectives on the same core concerns—agency and authenticity.

You've got the Westerns, the crime genre Eastern-Westerns, you've got the other crime novels. Within the crime books, you've got the Catholic books. You've got the sort of *National Geographic* books, like the ones that take place in Cuba and Nicaragua, partially, or Djibouti, or Italy. They're not isolated as islands, they all cover areas of interest that are recognizably Elmore Leonard's.

There's this sort of autobiographical series with *The Hot Kid* (2005), *Comfort to the Enemy* (2006), and *Up in Honey's Room* (2007). *The Hot Kid*, which is based on the gangsters that were in the news when he was a kid, then we move to Nazis in American prison camps, then we move to an immediate post–World War II Detroit context. It's kind of a rough trilogy in which Leonard himself doesn't appear but issues and things of interest to him in his life appear.

He published a book every year or every two years. He didn't have the luxury of setting aside ten years and saying, "This is going to be my masterpiece." I think he felt as though he didn't want to do anything that was radically different in terms of methods. Maybe *Djibouti* is the most radical, in terms of his jimmying around with chronology. Otherwise, no, he's not the kind of writer that would write a masterpiece, or even think of writing one. That's pretty much true of most crime writers. Take some of the greatest, like Raymond Chandler or Dashiell Hammett. For Hammett some might say *The Glass Key* (1930) is the masterpiece. Others would say *The Maltese Falcon* (1930) is the masterpiece. Some would say for Chandler it's *The Big Sleep* (1939). "Well, I'm a fan of *Farewell, My Lovely*" (1940). "No, no, no, it's *The Long Goodbye*" (1953). It's not like James Joyce where you publish three books in your whole life. Only three, and the unanimous choice is *Ulysses* (1922).

I think words like "masterwork" or "masterpiece" may be the problem here, not the quality of the book. Now that I think about it, how many writers would you say wrote a masterpiece? Something that puts everything else they wrote into the second tier? Maybe Tolstoy with *War and Peace* (1869). Even Dostoevsky—would you say it's *Crime and Punishment* (1866) or would you say it's *The Brothers Karamazov* (1880)? Or Hemingway—what's Hemingway's masterpiece?

I'm not trying to denigrate the question, but now that we're talking about it I wonder how often you can talk about anyone's masterpiece.

What made you decide to write the book Being Cool?

CJR: It came out of writing the essay for the *Companion to Crime Fiction*. By the time I'd finished that essay, I said, "Wow, I see a lot more going on here that I can't include in this essay. I want to explore this a little bit more." In order to write the essay, I read several more Leonard books. The more I read, the more I felt my initial thesis was confirmed. I could cite examples. But I also saw all this other stuff going on and I wanted to know more. And I began to think there was enough here to write a serious book about him. Then I set myself to reading everything he'd written. All of his stories. All of his novels. Then I set about reading them again. I've read everything he's ever written at least twice, and some things I've read three times. While I'm doing that, more and more questions arise, so I say, "I've got to talk to him about this!" That's when I tried to get in touch with him and ask if he had time for an interview.

14. Charles J. Rzepka

At the end of our first interview I said, "Would you mind meeting with me again so we could pursue some of these questions?" And he said, "Yeah, this was interesting. Stuff I hadn't thought about before." Then one thing led to another and we did the rest of the interviews. Some were by phone, and a lot of it became important source material for the book. When I was conducting the interviews, I was putting together first drafts of chapters and outlines and so forth.

Did Leonard get to see any of the book before he passed away?

CJR: Yes. I sent him the complete typescript. I don't know if I sent him the page proofs. I believe I did. He seemed to like it, had some advice about the title—which I took. But it was one of the greatest disappointments of my life that he died just days before ... no, *the* day of, if I'm not mistaken, the official release of the book.

You did a brief tribute to Leonard for NPR. How did that come about?

CJR: Initially, I was asked by Johns Hopkins University Press to write material for their blog that was related to Leonard. This NPR piece grew out of that request, but it wasn't part of it. I wrote it as a tribute and I began asking around to see who might be interested in publishing it. I asked my colleague at Boston University, John Carroll, in the School of Communication if he knew of a good place to send it. Carroll was a reporter and an opinion columnist here in Boston, and a television personality as well, a regular on NPR on one of their news shows. He suggested I get in touch with Frannie Toth, who's the editor of *Cognoscenti*. That's an online publication of NPR's Boston affiliate, WBUR. Frannie was interested. So that's how it ended up there.

The collection Charlie Martz and Other Stories: The Unpublished Stories *was published posthumously. You wrote about some of the stories in your book. What are your thoughts on the stories themselves and them being released posthumously?*

CJR: As a scholar, I'm delighted they were published. That's a really important source of information about Leonard's development as a writer, the range of interests he had over that early part of his career. There are a couple of them referred to in my book that I read when they were still in typescript. Leonard asked Greg Sutter to send the typescript to me and I read it through. I really enjoyed reading them and found a lot of them useful in supporting my points in the book.

So I welcome their publication.

Perspectives on Elmore Leonard

A lot has been talked about the academics sort of turning up their noses at Leonard earlier in his career. Why do you think that was?

CJR: I don't know if it was so much turning up their noses at him. I'd say he was largely neglected because, to put it simply, they weren't aware of him. They were aware if they were working on crime fiction—people like Geherin and James Devlin, his earliest biographers—but there were very few of those folks around in the '50s and '60s. Most people in academe get settled into a certain niche, a specialization, or a certain writer they take to, and they don't like to budge off of that. Despite his popularity with the general public, I don't think the right people had read Leonard in the academy. That's all. It's just a matter of serendipity. There are a lot of really good writers out there that deserve more credit and more attention from people like me in colleges and universities who are publishing scholarly articles or books on popular culture or on popular genres, whether we're talking about romance novels or adventure stories or crime novels. There's just so much out there, even if you pare it down to the big sellers and the most prominent writers. There are so many good writers out there! I think it's just a matter of you finding that writer, and something clicks. So I don't think it was a deliberate snub.

You were also asking about why all that—the lack of academic attention—changed later in his life. I don't know if I have an answer to that, either. Maybe it's like a snowball picking up a little momentum, moving downhill, picking up mass as it moves along. I hope my book had something to do with that, once it was published, and the articles I wrote on his work since his death. I had an article on *The Big Bounce*. I had another one on his early crime novels and this Odyssean-theme that appears in them, which I trace back to his earliest reading—his sister reading him the story of Odysseus from *My Book House* (1937), the collection of children's books that he mentions in the interviews. All that's given him some attention from academics.

There are also some shorter articles and now this collection of critical essays from Wiley called *Critical Essays on Elmore Leonard: If It Sounds Like Writing*. There was a special session at the Modern Language Association Convention a couple of years after he died that I sponsored, too. I'd like to think I had something to do with heightening his profile among my colleagues.

Leonard wrote and was published for parts of seven decades. What do you see as being the most significant changes in his style during his evolution as a writer? You told me earlier that you don't think his style changed dramatically, but there were some changes.

CJR: People often point to Elmore Leonard's own statement about the importance of George Higgins's *The Friends of Eddie Coyle* (1970). That did have a major impact on his writing. As I say in *Being Cool*, I think it mostly had to do with his way of conveying a sense of place. And his ear for the speaking voice. Higgins's ear is very finely tuned in that book, and people say, "Ah, that's where Leonard got interested in dialogue...." Uh-uh. The book itself consists of long monologues. There's hardly any dialogue, any conversational back-and-forth, there. But after reading Higgins, Leonard did start paying more attention to the speaking voice. I don't know if that's exactly where he got his "Panasonic ear," but in general, his earlier works are more prose-y. Even as late as *The Moonshine Wars* (1970) there are long paragraphs of description.

And then, a shift happens with *Mr. Majestyk*, which is written at about the same time as *The Moonshine War*. It's written as a screenplay that he turns into a book. That might have something to do with it. It even reads more as a screenplay. I think there's more dialogue, more back and forth, in that book than in *The Moonshine Wars*, and certainly more than in *The Big Bounce*.

Then from there, it's like he's hearing voices, characters speaking, whether to others or to themselves in their heads. In *52 Pickup* and *Swag*, it's like he's R&B-ing his way through the seventies—in the Detroit books generally. There's suddenly this ear that I don't really detect so prominently in the stuff before that. I'm just speculating here, based on your question. That to me might be the most important stylistic change, for whatever reason. He was not always the author with the Panasonic ear.

Will Leonard's work persevere? Will he still be read in 100 years?

CJR: I sure hope so! But I don't know. I really don't. Who from 100 years ago is still read today? Or maybe we should qualify that—read by *whom*? I hope Leonard will be read by academics and scholars who want to write about and teach him. I hope he'll still appear on the syllabus. That's where most writers who were once popular manage to survive. Who reads a Joseph Conrad book, nowadays? I think mostly people in college, or with college educations. There are just a few classic crime writers from a century ago—we're talking before 1920, right?—who are still in print and read universally by crime fiction fans, and you can name them on the fingers of one hand—actually, just two fingers: Doyle and Christie (who started in 1920), and maybe a third for Edgar Allan Poe's August Dupin. I don't know that a lot of ordinary readers check a book out of the library by Joseph Conrad. I don't know if many general readers will be checking out Elmore Leonard in a hundred years, either. I hope they will though. My hope is that people like me will continue writing about him and make him interesting to new generations of readers, students, future scholars, and maybe he'll enter the pantheon at some point and appear as a regular or semi-regular entry on a syllabus of writers, and people will still be putting together essay anthologies about him. I sure hope so.

15

Daniel Schecter

Daniel Schecter is a film director, screenwriter, and editor. After helming two short films, he wrote the screenplay for the Ishai Setton-directed indie film *The Big Bad Swim* (2006). He then made his feature directorial debut with *Goodbye Baby* (2007). He followed that with *Supporting Characters* (2012), his second film as director.

Now having directed two well-reviewed dramas, Schecter set his sites on adapting Elmore Leonard's novel *The Switch* (1978). An admirer of Quentin Tarantino's *Rum Punch* (1992) adaptation *Jackie Brown* (1997), Schecter liked the idea of making a sort of prequel to that (*The Switch* featured the first appearances of characters Ordell Robbie, Louis Gara, and Melanie Ralston). Schecter adapted the novel himself, re-titling it *Life of Crime* (2013). He cast Yasiin Bey (Mos Def) and John Hawkes as the leads. He managed to snag Jennifer Aniston to play the kidnapped wife Mickey Dawson. Aniston then came onboard as a producer, helping Schecter find the necessary funding. The film would ultimately feature such talents as Tim Robbins, Isla Fisher, Will Forte, and Mark Boone, Jr., in supporting roles. The film premiered on closing night at the Toronto International Film Festival.

Schecter has since followed *Life of Crime* with the film *After Class* (2019), which he also wrote.

ANDREW J. RAUSCH: *You've said in the past that* Get Shorty *(1990) was the first Elmore Leonard novel that you read. How old were you when you read that and what was your reaction to the material at that time?*

DANIEL SCHECTER: I think I was seventeen years old. It was right before I left for college and I was such a lousy reader that the only books I'd ever allow myself to pick up were ones based on movies that I liked, because I was far more into film than reading. Like every other novel of Leonard's that I've read since, you read literally the first paragraph and you're hooked and you can't put it down. He's sort of a double-edged sword with him being a gateway drug to reading. On one level, it definitely made me a much more avid reader because he was the first person who gave me great pleasure reading a book. On the other hand, I have never really enjoyed reading anyone else as much as I enjoyed reading his novels. Especially people within the same genre. I was never able to find that same high that I got from his work. He was literally my favorite writer and I found him right out of the gate.

In hindsight, I would say *Get Shorty* is my favorite novel of his. I think it's pretty close to perfection and is a masterpiece. And the more I get involved in the industry of filmmaking, the more I'm around artists, and the more I personally try to create stories, the more I realize just how insanely well-observed a book it is. But at the same time, with every chapter, you're excited to see what that character is doing. It's a brilliant satire. I even recently watched the television series and got sucked into the first season because it was just such an intoxicating premise. This gangster that loved movies who just wanted to do that but had a certain skill set that translated is still one of the greatest premises ever, and the execution is, I think, perfection. Somehow the book more so than the movie version of *Get Shorty*. It's not quite as satirical as you would think. Even the portrayal of Martin Weir, which I know was based on Dustin Hoffman; there's a lot of respect for that person, while in the movie it's pretty much just a straight up parody of an artist drunk on success. When you read the way Chili observes Weir in the book, there's a lot of reverence for him and he acknowledges him as a remarkably talented person, while at the same time, being a huge pain in the ass.

What made you want to adapt The Switch?

DS: I would imagine the same is true for all filmmakers in that you pick up a book of his and you start drafting a screenplay immediately and you hope this is the one that will inspire you to want to fight for it and that it will be adaptable. But then most books, even the ones I love a lot, tend to veer off into something that won't quite work. They're either too long, or it's awkwardly shaped, or the ending isn't as climatic and perfect as you want it to be. Because, as I'm sure you're aware, Leonard doesn't plan much past the third or fifth chapter and he really allows the characters to take over. *The Switch* had everything.

First of all, just as a practical, independent filmmaker, it's not a huge movie. It's a very small, almost Hitchcock-ian, DePalma-esque esque that was really isolated to five or six major locations. That immediately made it appealing. And, of course, it had the same characters as my favorite adaptation, *Jackie Brown*. That made it tantalizing, just as a

it from a book. But that was a perfect-sized book. But people feel they need to prove their worth by changing things.

I mean, I loved the book *Be Cool* (1999). I thought *Be Cool* was an awesome sequel. And then when you watch the movie, it is almost the greatest parody of all time regarding how badly you can fuck up an Elmore Leonard adaptation. You're taking, what I thought, was a pretty great Elmore Leonard villain and turning him into the truly cringe-worthy Vince Vaughn character. That's probably the ultimate example of how badly you can do. And it was a pretty decent set-up but there was something about the casual cool of the book that was thrown out. On every level, everyone made a mistake on that. It bummed me out. I would've loved that assignment. It's also really insightful as to how the music industry works and how people have to sell their souls. There was even a really sweet romance between Chili and one of the movie executives. But it wasn't sensational, and I guess that's really something they couldn't stand. That one broke my heart more than all of the others.

According to producer Lee Stollman, Leonard said your adaptation was the best adaptation of his work by anyone not named Scott Frank or Quentin Tarantino. What is your reaction to that?

DS: If you take me at my word about how little I did with the script, you could take it as him just saying, "Oh, he did a good job like a doctor—he first did no harm. He didn't undo something that was working in the original book." And I would say that was true. It wasn't for lack of creativity. I do think it was a humility on my part that realized, "This is pretty good." There were a couple of things I invented. There was a sequence I wrote where Marshall goes to see the Richard Monk character at the house because I wanted to keep that Marshall story-line alive. This guy is trying to have an affair. He witnesses the kidnapping and he's in a horrible moral dilemma. I thought, "That's funny, and this guy disappears for the rest of the book. I want to see him squirm." And then I wanted a bit more action in the movie, and that's one of the few moments of pride where you're almost doing fan fiction with characters that are beloved, and yet it made total organic sense to the movie and it raised the stakes. That was one of the few moments where I thought, "Oh, maybe if Leonard had thought of this he would've written that out." And it worked for the story; it added to the story and it didn't take away from everything else that was working.

Of course you have to trim things out and there's not much that I missed from the original, although I'll occasionally open the book and go, "Damn, that was a good line!" Or "Damn, that was a good scene," but it probably would've gotten cut in editing because you have to shape it to the organic size of a film. I would put that compliment back onto him. He just saw I didn't go crazy with it and the way I honored the original material.

You've said that you were intimidated by the thought of adapting Leonard's work because you didn't want to disappoint him. Would you like to talk about that?

DS: That is true and I stand by it one hundred percent. The heartbreaking thing was, I remember I had shown him a sizzle reel at one point. It was something we cut together after production to show the cast and crew and some investors that we had some cool stuff. He had seen that and he was really pleased with it. Then he heard that we were going to play on closing night of the Toronto Film Festival, which was really big news for everybody. I think he hadn't had a prestigious win like that in a little while, so he asked to watch it. Like all filmmakers I said, "Give me two more weeks. I'll have the sound, the color, the music, and it'll all be done and I can really show you something special." And, of course, he had his stroke in that time and then he passed away two weeks later. It was a really rapid decline. It was sort of a sick, really sad joke.

However, if I'm being blunt with you, he was an incredibly ornery man at that age. I think he would've been more likely to find a hole in the doughnut rather than appreciate the doughnut itself. He was very critical of just about everything. Even Tarantino's film, as I understand it; apparently it took him a moment to come around to see how great it was. And I've had that. I've had one or two scripts produced by other people, and it's a freakish experience to watch it the first time. It's very overwhelming to see someone else's choices with your work, and it does take time—sometimes years—to allow the dust to settle and objectively see it for what it is. So my guess is, he would've had more criticisms than praise at first. The people closest to him seem to feel that we were in that upper group that did a decent job and not the ones that they have to apologize for. I probably more or less agree that we're in the upper-middle half of the adaptations.

You said you're a big fan of Quentin Tarantino's—

DS: I revere Tarantino as a filmmaker as much as I do Leonard as a novelist. I truly think he's the greatest talent working today and there's no one I admire more. It was intimidating kind of swimming in his waters. There's a great story that you may have heard where, as a kid, he picked up *The Switch*—the book I adapted—and apparently pocketed the book, got caught, and then went back and stole it again. Without question I think, despite his billions of influences, there's no way anyone influenced Tarantino more than Leonard. It's just so plainly obvious when you watch his work that his biggest influence is Leonard.

Your film is, in essence, a prequel to Jackie Brown.

DS: I don't know if Tarantino ever saw my movie, but I went up to him after a screening of *The Hateful Eight* (2015). There was a long line of glad-handers or whatever and I said, "Hey, I did that movie, the one that was kind of a prequel to *Jackie Brown* called *Life of Crime*." He said, "Ah man, you did that? I haven't seen it yet! Sam [Jackson] and I really wanted to watch it!" Again, I don't know if he watched it and was being polite.... Then I kind of slunk away, but I got the sense I could've said, "Hey, you wanna grab a drink?," and he would've been excited. But I kind of get nervous to talk to people like that. He kept kind of side-eyeing me after that and I thought, "Oh, maybe he wants me to stick around," because he was talking to awkward people. I always regret that moment in my life because I do think we could've gone and had a really cool chat.

I think the lack of success of *Life of Crime*, to me, it wasn't like a bomb. Most people didn't even know it existed. The company that bought it was Lionsgate. We sold it in Toronto and that was a big accomplishment in my life. Then I think they had not-so-great test screening or something like that, and they edited a cruddy trailer and then put it literally in two or three theaters in America. Then it went away forever. I think it's on Amazon Prime now, so some people talk about it, but it was such a bummer. It could've done well. I think Aniston is fucking great in it! I adored working with her. I was cautious working with her at first, but then she wildly over-delivered and it felt fun to see her do something outside of the genre she's most comfortable in. I think she was a great casting choice for Mickey Dawson.

You might also know this story to *The Switch*. Famously, Leonard met his wife and sobered up around the time he wrote *The Switch*. I think the two great influences she had on him was sobering him and the book, which is absolutely about his being an alcoholic and how toxic he was as a husband. And she really encouraged him to write stronger female characters, and I think Mickey Dawson was his first terrific female character. He then went on to write many great characters from that point of view. She is such a fully fleshed-out persona. Most of the book you're in her mindset. It's an absolutely pleasure.

There's some female empowerment themes in the book in terms of the progression of Mickey's character. Was that an element of the story that interested you?

DS: Oh, without question. That is the absolute arc of the movie that is so deeply satisfying. She is someone whom I can relate to even as a guy. Someone who is constantly suppressing every clever thought or anger that she has inside of her. And by the end of it, it's so satisfying to watch her go toe to toe with the Tim Robbins character, and I adore that about it.

But someone that has no arc and is just immediately a force of nature is the Melanie character that is done in a different way in *Jackie Brown*. I think that was one of the areas where we veered off. The original character was much more bohemian. I think Tarantino turned her into a bit more of a California beach bunny stoner type. But she is by far the smartest character and has the most delicious dialogue in the entire piece. Every actress in town wanted to play that part because she's a woman in her twenties who is sexy, smart as hell, fiendish, and has great control over the narrative of the story. She's a really delicious character, and there aren't many like that. She was just such a pleasure to write for and examine her motivations which changed like the wind. She was great.

Without question I think Mickey and Melanie are the most exciting characters. I think if it was just a Louis and Ordell prequel I wouldn't have done it. It was having Mickey at the heart of it and having this antagonist in Melanie that really made the book special.

Jackie Brown *and* Life of Crime *are completely different films. You talked about the change in Melanie.... Were there any aspects of Tarantino's film that you sought to approach differently, or were there any aspects of that film that you were interested in mimicking?*

DS: There's a great line in *Jackie Brown*. I'm not sure if it's from the book or not, and sometimes Tarantino would slightly alter specific lines. Ordell says to Louis, "What happened to you, man? You used to be beautiful." That's what he says. We're meeting a much more burnt-out version of Louis by the time we meet him in *Rum Punch*. I think that was the goal. The goal was, if these two movies are watched side by side, they should be made by different filmmakers. I probably stole more from the Coen brothers, visually, than Tarantino's style. I remember wanting to deliver on that promise. Who was this guy before he did probably several long stints in jail and really became burnt out? And I love John Hawkes. I love his performance. I always say he's sort of like Charlie Chaplin in that film if Chaplin was a criminal. There's a lovable tramp quality, but you also would not want to get into a scrape with him. There's still sort of a criminal underneath. He was known for doing half of his characters like the one he plays in *Winter's Bone* (2010) and then half that were really sweet, avuncular like his *Me and You and Everyone We Know* (2005) and *Deadwood* characters. I thought, this guy is right in the middle. He could really capture both. I was much more interested in what the younger version of Louis was than Ordell because, in this version, you can see Ordell maybe trying to get out of being a pimp and moving to drugs or weapons and trying to create an industry for himself. It's the first time we see Ordell grapple with the moral dilemma of murder for furthering himself. I believe the first time he considers murder is in this story when he uses the rich as a proxy for himself to murder the Mickey Dawson character.

Overall, the reason I loved *Jackie Brown* was that it felt like reading an Elmore Leonard novel. I loved hanging with those characters. I prefer *Jackie Brown* more now when I can watch it on Netflix or DVD and I can pause it and maybe watch the rest of it later. Like the book, it's a hair long. But I wouldn't cut a single scene from it. I totally adore it. And now I watch it all the way through because I have so much affection built in for those characters.

I think [Tarantino] got it right; He recognized that it wasn't just about the plot points. It was like, oh, we love hanging out with Max Cherry and watching him go to the movies or flirt with Jackie. I knew I would never come close to that movie and it wasn't the goal. I wanted to deliver something else entirely. His is a much more mature film in a lot of ways, meaning that it has the maturity to sit back and relax and trust that the audience will anticipate the action and we can just have long talking scenes. I don't have his depth as a screenwriter. I just don't. Nor do I have, I think, the audiences' will to let me be indulgent. As a younger, less mature filmmaker, I was more trying to mix in as much action with the dialogue of the characters as possible. Which is the way people go wrong with Elmore Leonard. There's not a tremendous amount of action. It comes every three or four chapters. You'll get a punch or a murder or something like that, but mostly, it's long, wonderful conversations. I was in the shadow of that film without a doubt. That was certainly daunting.

Because of the restraint and maturity he showed with that film, people didn't know what to make of it when it was first released. The feel of the movie is so different from Reservoir Dogs *(1992) or* Pulp Fiction *(1994).* Jackie Brown *has more of a Leonard dynamic than what you would consider a Tarantino dynamic.*

DS: It seems to have aged well. Most people, I think, really revere it and put it up there. I really didn't like it at first, but after *Pulp Fiction* I think people just didn't know what to expect. But also it's different, even by today's standards. How many films have two people who are around 50 as the leads? In a crime movie. Even that is such a bold choice. If I could go back and tell myself anything, it would be that Tarantino just made it so personal. It really felt like a half Tarantino/half Elmore Leonard thing. And you can see Tarantino's fetishes in it, his personal relationships in it, and yet he somehow kept it directly on track with what the Elmore Leonard book would have wanted to deliver. It's masterful what he pulls off! It's reverent yet he added something. I didn't add as much, probably to a fault. I think now my other work is more personal and I remind myself to do that every time.

Tarantino has a great line when he talks about doing another Elmore adaptation. He goes, "You know, I think what I was born to do was to create these worlds and these characters. If I didn't exist, the Aldo Raine character wouldn't exist, the Vince Vega character wouldn't exist. Django wouldn't exist. And that's what I was put here to do." And I think in my own humble way, that's kind of what I'm doing now. More small, personal comedies that I have a bit more authority over that truly would not exist if I didn't. I think Joel and Ethan Coen could've done a great job directing *The Switch* and it might have had more added to it and maybe better than mine. I do think that's the lesson I got out of it, but I do feel like I got to go to some kind of fantasy baseball camp or something and play with the most unbelievable material. I was writing a thriller at the time and then I picked up *The Switch* and go, "Oh, this is a much tighter and better version of what I'm trying to do and so therefore I would much rather do this novel."

I can't overstate how much I think *Jackie Brown* is an absolute masterpiece.

I read an interview you did with John Hawkes where he said he hadn't read Rum Punch *and he hadn't seen* Jackie Brown *so he had no idea his character was eventually going to die. I thought that was funny.*

DS: Leonard famously said that, and I always found that line daunting as well. He said when he wrote *The Switch* he knew one of these two guys would kill the other, but he didn't know who. Until he wrote *Rum Punch*, and then I think he made the right and logical choice. I think Louis was a much more morally ambiguous character and he had a much more difficult time justifying crime than Ordell did. I think Ordell was more of a sociopath. It was hit or miss. He really couldn't stand by and let harm come to this woman. And it's sweetly in the same sense as Max Cherry and Jackie Burke—he has a crush on her! And sometimes it's that simple. That's my favorite part of Elmore Leonard. As soon as there's a love interest, you can't wait to get back to it. He has a way of just making you hunger for those two people to have a conversation. It's a protagonist and the antagonist having a conversation, but he makes you incredibly starved for the conversation between the two characters; you are dying to get them into a room together. It's a great gift. It's always an enormously pleasurable tale.

It's very similar to Out of Sight—*the dynamic between the female good person and the male bad guy.*
   DS: That was the theme I found in *The Switch* the more I went over and over it that I was personally relating to, which is just men throwing away all logic with abandon for a woman that they had an infatuation with. And that's true of the husband with Melanie, the Louis character with Mickey, that's true of the Marshall character—they're all making decisions based on an infatuation. I think maybe more so men than women, you don't question that motive because every guy has lost their mind temporarily to see how far he can get with a woman he wants.

You talked about Leonard being kind of ornery. You met him a couple times. What were your experiences with him like?
   DS: I only met him one time. I went to go to Bloomfield Hills, Michigan. It was like a movie when a fanboy goes to meet his celebrity crush and he's just unabashedly quoting him and reminding him of things. It was like the Chris Farley character on *SNL*. And the things I was referencing, he didn't remember. He was older. It wasn't like meeting Muhammad Ali in his prime.
   I think he always went into an adaptation of his work with extreme caution, but there was this underlying hope of "please make me a good one I can be proud of." It was very hard. He had been burned too many times and I think you could feel that the walls were up. You were guilty until proven innocent. The difference at this point in his life was, and

I don't know how he was throughout his life, he wanted money! There was a financial motivation towards adaptations being made. I think at that point he was somebody who was thinking about his legacy, what he would pass on to his family, stuff like that. There was always a sense that was a really big motivator for him. And by the way, it felt great when I was able to get the movie financed—which is really difficult to do these days, even with Jennifer Aniston as the lead—and could give him more reward for creating great material and would expose more people to his work, which is always the goal because he has such an impact on my life.

He certainly wasn't rude or shitty in any way. I just felt more familiar with his body of work than he was. [Laughs.] There was too much of it. He hadn't read some of it in thirty or forty years. And he was an older guy.

How did you get Jennifer Aniston to help finance the film?

DS: It's really, really hard to get a film financed now. I thought, oh, once we get Jennifer Aniston, we're going to get this eleven, ten million dollar movie financed like a snap, because that's what you get paid to do for a movie. This should be easy. But it took a year! I think for investors, it was gamble; her doing a movie outside of her romantic comedy genre was far less financially reliable than her doing something in that genre. However, creatively it was really exciting to get to show her doing something totally different. That's the payoff from my point of view, but they weren't really enthusiastic about it.

It's not like somebody that auditions for you. I didn't even make an offer to her. To me, that was too ambitious. Her people came to us. I'm too pragmatic. We heard she might be interested and I thought, well, that could be really cool if it's done well. But you don't really know until the first day of shooting how good she's going to be. Then I remember being on set thinking, this person is a mega-talent who can do anything. She did anything I asked without ego, without question, with everything she had. She loved the physical scenes. She loved being kidnapped or being attacked by Richard because there's no acting there! She was able to be terrified and let herself be carried away, and I thought she was incredibly compelling in those scenes. And then it was fun to see her be girlishly flirty, putting her head on Louis' hand and saying, "I want to go home now." I was really in awe of her. I'm still eager to work with her again. I always love seeing an actor do something they haven't done before. I think she really delivered on that.

There's a chunk of the movie where she has to wear a blindfold. Did she balk at any that?

DS: No. As I said, my impression of her was that whenever she didn't have to "act"—for example, stumbling through a room with a blindfold on or not knowing where the person was standing in a room with her—removes a lot of the artificial bullshit she had to do. I think things like that gave her something to focus on and do that made it more real for her.

You had a fantastic cast, top to bottom. Did any of them express that they were fans of Elmore Leonard?

DS: I wish I could say the answer was yes, [but] no, not really. I don't believe there was anybody there that had the same reverence I had. There's a great picture, though, of me and Tim Robbins on set that somebody took. He has the book open in front of him and I have a laptop. We said it was like legal plagiarism; we were just stealing lines because it was such great material and we didn't have to invent anything. And he loved the character so much and loved the writing so much that he would do that. Same thing with Aniston. I remember one night before a shoot she was reading the chapters and she said, "Can we put these four or five lines back in where I'm talking to my son?" And I said yes. I think she loved that because you can't really do that on a studio movie, but on an independent film you can. That was really liberating.

The actors were reading the book as we went through it. I bought thirty copies of *The Switch* off of Amazon just to hand out to literally anyone on the cast and crew who wanted to read it. I think my goal was to say, "I want to make this. This is the exact tone and world I want to do and I want you to know the movie we're making." The production designer, the costume designer, an actor, a sound person, whatever; I wanted everyone to read that book.

Charlie Stella

Charlie Stella was born Carmelo Stella, the son of a "knock-around guy," in Manhattan, New York. After being raised in Brooklyn and attending Canarsie High School, Stella received a football scholarship to attend Minot State College in North Dakota. During his sophomore year, he discovered author George V. Higgins' debut novel, *The Friends of Eddie Coyle* (1970). Just as it had done with Elmore Leonard, *The Friends of Eddie Coyle* had a significant impact on Stella. Where the novel inspired Leonard to change his style a bit, focusing more on realistic street dialogue, it inspired Stella to become a crime writer.

Stella followed in his father's footsteps, becoming a knockaround guy himself for a period. No doubt this would eventually play a significant role in his writing. After writing some off-Broadway plays, he published his first novel, *Eddie's World* in 2001. He then followed that with nine more novels (to date) including *Jimmy Bench-Press* (2002), *Charlie Opera* (2010), and *Johnny Porno* (2010). His novels have all been well-reviewed and his sharp dialogue-driven writing is frequently compared to that of Elmore Leonard and George V. Higgins. Stella is also a fan of Leonard's work.

In 2015, Stella wrote James Guiliani's memoir, *Dogfella: How an Abandoned Dog Named Bruno Turned This Mobster's Life Around*. Guiliani was also from the street and was a member of John Gotti, Jr.'s crew.

ANDREW J. RAUSCH: *Throughout your career your dialogue has been compared to that of Elmore Leonard and George V. Higgins. Were they both influences?*

CS: Yeah, absolutely. Higgins came first for me. I attended college in North Dakota on a football scholarship. An English teacher, Dave Gresham, actually started a class one day by reading the beginning of *The Friends of Eddie Coyle* (1970). It hooked me because it was like, "Holy shit! I know people who talk like that." Then he had me read *Glitz* by Elmore Leonard, and that was another book that influenced me.

16. Charlie Stella

I hadn't been much of a reader until college, so it was all new to me and a great find. I really liked their styles and how they put the reader in the moment.

You're a fan of both, but a little bit more of a fan of Higgins, who actually inspired Leonard. For you, how do you compare their styles, and what do you prefer about Higgins'?

CS: The difference between the two, for me, has to do with introspection. In Higgins, it's very narrow. It's more of a theater feel. More like a play or movie script. Not much introspection. With Leonard there's much more introspection and I suppose most people prefer it that way. Leonard is good at it. He can keep your interest. I've read everything by Higgins. I haven't read everything by Leonard, but I've read most of his work. Higgins, after his third book, once he became political, it was difficult to follow him. His first three books to me are three of the greatest crime novels ever. I can't read back-to-back Leonard because at some point the introspection bothers me. If I wait long enough, Leonard's work is sublime. I just can't read more than a book at a time with Leonard.

There are still some readers and critics that have this conception that language in literature should always be formal. But as we know, people don't talk like that in real life. As someone who writes in more of an informal style, what are your thoughts on that?

CS: You write how and what works for you, the writer. It's nonsense to stick to any rules that inhibit your work. There are writers, great writers like the late Hubert Selby, Jr., who would make your head spin if what you're looking for is formal writing. I just discovered a great writer who I'd never heard of before. Jose Saramago is dead now, but he won the Nobel Prize for literature based on his collective works. I received one of his most popular books, *Blindness*, as a gift and then read two more by him back to back. Like Selby, he doesn't pay attention to the formal code. There is no punctuation and sentences start and stop when you see a capital letter. They can go on for pages, yet you don't miss a thing. As for writing about street guys, they generally come from a blue collar world. If you want to portray their vernacular, you can forget the rulebooks. Same goes for anyone offended by the characters, how they behave, and so on. They aren't politically correct, even the more liberal ones, and they certainly wouldn't concern themselves with what might earn them a demerit from the cancel culture. They'll use words that many find extremely offensive, but my suggestion to those offended is to avoid it if it upsets you. But if you're the writer and you want to be true to what you're writing, you'll have to ignore those who get offended. Cunt, twat, gash, nigger, spic, etc., are still some of the words tossed around by some of the characters we might read or write. I think it's great that I don't see or hear those words as much today as when I was growing up, but if you're writing about the kinds of characters who do use such language, I don't see how you avoid it.

It's an absurd idea that political correctness should be interjected into this when that isn't realistic in that world. You don't look to knockaround guys for highly-enlightened views on society. You wouldn't look to them to find political correctness. I just find that idea ridiculous.

CS: It's as absurd as America electing a complete moron for President, only more so. Associates are the bottom of the barrel when it comes to knockaround guys. The actual vernacular designates them as a "nobody," even after they've been spoken for. While there are surely some in that world who can read and write and give informed opinions on whatever, the bulk are clueless as the day is long about anything outside of their immediate purview. That said, most do know the difference between right and wrong, what is moral and what isn't. People make choices for any number of reasons the same as they find the justification for their choices. It's the part of my life I'm ashamed of to this day. I knew what I was doing was wrong and immoral, but I allowed the money to own me. I've spent the last 20 plus years trying to make up for it, and it is within those 20 plus years when I remembered the importance of education. I can give you my two-cents on most subjects, but that's what it'd be worth, about two cents.

You're not going to pontificate on Jean-Paul Sartre.

CS: Well, I might, but the company I used to keep sure wasn't. I was telling this to someone the other day: there was a former partner of mine, we were driving together and he happened to say to me, it just was around V-E Day or whatever, it came on the radio and he turned to me and said, "What the hell is that?" I said, "You should be smacked." We both had a good laugh, even after I explained it to him. [Laughs.]

I guess that explains why your work comes across as being so authentic.

CS: It was a bad choice in life. It's not all that romantic and it's dangerous whether one realizes it or not. Dangerous because of the cut-throats you're dealing with and dangerous because you can wind up in prison. For a while I did a little loan sharking, what I'm most ashamed of to this day, and a little book-making, so I know those worlds pretty well. It's not the crap you read about where guys are getting their legs broken. That's a crock of shit. Those are so rare it's ridiculous. People want to get their money. Only assholes would do something like that.

I was writing before I turned to the street and then my current wife finally got me off the street for good. She encouraged me to write again. I always took shots at it. I had a couple plays produced early on off, off–Broadway. And eventually I took a shot with a book and I got lucky. From that point on, it was an easy decision to walk away from the street, although my wife wouldn't have married me if I hadn't walked away. It was a lot of gelt to give up, but all you had to do was read the papers to see the dead end a street life was. Now I look at those years as a waste of time. I could've done so much more for people other than myself.

One of the things I admire about Leonard is his knack for describing his characters through the dialogue of other characters, which in turn allows him to characterize both characters simultaneously without exposition. As an author, how does that technique strike you?

CS: Like I said, he's so good at injecting introspection, sometimes you don't realize that it isn't dialogue. He was a master and we're all just trying our best by comparison. When I wrote after reading a Leonard novel, I found myself using introspection. In rereading, I realized I wasn't comfortable with what I was doing, mimicking Leonard. By the time I made it to a final draft, or tossed it aside, I wound up taking most of the introspection out. I understand it. I think it's great. I love reading it when he does it. But as a writer, I couldn't sustain it. In other words, I'd do it and I'd see myself getting carried away and I'd have to go in and edit a lot of it out. But when Leonard did it, it was brilliant.

Are there any things in your last draft writing that you see as being influenced directly by Leonard?

CS: I probably started every crime novel I ever wrote with a line of dialogue or a line of dialogue that became the theme of the book. I stopped writing straight crime fiction over the past two years. I don't even read as much of it as I used to, so my last few projects were heavily influenced by more literary fiction. That said, I've also grown used to some introspection I'm finding necessary for the tales I now tell, so that's Leonard for sure ... and I probably should pick up one of the Leonard novels I haven't read. I'm sure I wouldn't be disappointed.

What do you think it is about Leonard that made him a bigger commercial success than Higgins?

CS: I think Higgins' first book was rejected like fifty times, and then it took off as a national best-seller, and then you never heard of him again by comparison to Leonard. He kept writing, but it was never going to be *The Friends of Eddie Coyle*. I think Leonard is just more palatable. I think because of the introspection he mastered and the subject matter and its affinity with going to the big screen. Think about the titles alone. *Glitz, Swag, Pronto, Get Shorty, Be Cool*, etc. They're perfect for the movies. Eddie Coyle made it to the big screen and it was great, but until *Cogan's Trade* was done a few years back with Brad Pitt and James Gandolfini, retitled "Killing Them Softly," it was too late for Higgins. He'd been dead awhile by then. And once Higgins turned away from crime writing because his ego couldn't handle being labeled a crime novelist, he wrote stuff that was very difficult for readers to absorb. I know I had major problems with some of his later books. Until he returned to basic crime in *A Year or So with Edgar*, there was a long dry spell for him (at least for me).

Higgins and Leonard both wrote in a style that would seem conducive to screen adaptation. However, their film adaptations often fail to capture the feeling of their work. Why do you think it's so hard capturing the essence of the books in the adaptations?

CS: I don't know. See above. *The Friends of Eddie Coyle* with Robert Mitchum, I love. I like the movie as much as the book. The other one, *Killing Them Softly* (2012) was a piece of shit movie compared to the book or the Eddie Coyle movie. That was just a piece of shit. But the book was great! The book is so good. It was one of Higgins' first three books and it wasn't called *Killing Them Softly*. It was called *Cogan's Trade* (1974).

Leonard, I haven't seen very many of his. I've seen three or four. *Jackie Brown* (1997), I saw. That was kind of fluffy to me. One with Charles Bronson I can't remember the name of. I don't know why Leonard's films don't do as well as the books, but I suspect it has to do with the comedy involved and the fluff Hollywood seems to prefer to portray. I really don't know. In Leonard's case, you can't do that same type of introspection. *Pronto* (1993) is one of my favorite Leonard books, and they did a good job with the movie. I think they got that one and *Get Shorty* right. But I think that introspection is a lot harder to portray in film. What Hollywood did with *Be Cool* was make it a joke while removing, at least for me, the tension the book provided. With Higgins, I just think they fucked up when they modernized *Cogan's Trade*. I think they should've left it [in the seventies].

Do you believe Elmore Leonard's work will still be read in fifty or a hundred years, and why or why not?

CS: That's so hard. [Laughs.] That's such a hard question. The way this world is going now, I don't know if humans will be around in a hundred years. But assuming they are, I don't think so. It's not because of a lack of talent. Times change. Tastes change. Fifth Avenue still has such an influence on everything that is sold. I can't imagine anything in literature of any sort will live on that long. I guess people will have classics from the literary world shoved down their throats, but even some of those have diminished over time.

I take a course every Tuesday night at Brooklyn Public Library. One of my political heroes teaches a course on Supreme Court decisions. And not just in that class, but I meet some people sometimes who've never read *The Grapes of Wrath* (1939). It's staggering to me how many people can get through life without reading a book like that. It took me many years to read it and understand it all (by rereading it twice more), but how can people ever appreciate the genius of a John Steinbeck if he's forgotten?

Fifty years from now, who knows if John Steinbeck will be the literary giant he should be. I wonder if his work is taught now.

Having actually spent time around street criminals, do Elmore Leonard's characters feel authentic to you in the way that Higgins' do?

Totally. He's got the patois down across the board for criminals and law enforcement alike. When I think about the bookmaker in *Pronto*, Jesus Christ, I knew so many guys just like that. Same goes for the muscle trying to pronounce *stroonz* in that book and the movie. Part of Leonard's legacy will be the fact he never let his characters down. From the bad-asses to the comical versions like Ray Bones (there are lots of Ray Bones types out there, at least there used to be).

17

Graham Yost

Born in Etobicoke, Ontario, in 1959, Graham Yost is the son of Canadian television personality Elwy Yost. He attended the University of Toronto Schools and Trinity College at the University of Toronto. He received his first screenwriting credit on the horror film *The Chair* (1988). He found work as a screenwriter and script consultant for two years on the television series *Hey Dude*. After that, he knocked around penning episodes for several series, but his real breakthrough came when he wrote the Jan de Bont thriller *Speed* (1994), which became a smash hit.

He then wrote the John Woo actioner *Broken Arrow* (1996), which was also a tremendous hit. In 1998, Yost worked as executive producer, screenwriter (of two episodes), and director (one episode) on the Tom Hanks/Ron Howard-produced mini-series *From the Earth to the Moon* (1998). He then worked with Hanks a second time, writing two episodes for Hanks' and Steven Spielberg's mini-series *Band of Brothers* (2001). He would then reunite with Hanks and Spielberg, working as a writer and director on the mini-series *The Pacific* (2010).

Yost created and executive produced two series, *Boomtown* and *Raines*, before creating the popular series *Justified* (2010–2015), which was based on Elmore Leonard's short story *Fire in the Hole* (2002). (Raylan Givens, the series' protagonist, is also featured in the Leonard novels *Pronto* [1993], *Riding the Rap* [1995], and *Raylan* [2011].)

Subsequently, Yost has served as executive producer on the series *Falling Skies* (2011), *The Americans* (2013), and *Sneaky Pete* (2019).

ANDREW J. RAUSCH: *When did you first become aware of the work of Elmore Leonard?*

GRAHAM YOST: The way I remember it was, I was reading a *New York Times* book review in the eighties. I think it was a review of *LaBrava* (1983). And if I'm not mistaken, I went out and bought it in hardcover, and I was not a successful, young man at that point, so buying a hardcover meant something to me. But it wasn't just that review. It was one of those things where I had been hearing about this guy for awhile. There was something in the ether about him being the coolest, best crime fiction writer. That intrigued me. I had read a lot of [Raymond] Chandler and [Dashiell] Hammett when I was a young guy, some [James M.] Cain. I read a certain amount of crime fiction, and there was something about the review saying how different it was, and sparkling, and fun. So I got *LaBrava* and that's where I started. I think over the next 20 years, I bought pretty much every one of his books that came out. Once we started doing the show, it was a deeper dive into ones I hadn't read, like *The Hunted* (1977) and *Swag* (1976) and *Gold Coast* (1980).

In your mind, what is it that makes Elmore Leonard unique as a writer?

GY: I think his love of his characters. If he gets a kick out of a character, you can tell that he's having fun and that the characters are having fun with each other. As he noted, they say very humorous things but they never crack a joke. People don't laugh, but they look at each other and it's that connection; that feeling of, "Oh, we're on the same wavelength." As soon as you get these two characters, especially a man and a woman, and they start do that dance, it's just so enjoyable! The seduction. The fun of it. There's a sort of jaded, slightly dark view of the world that these people have, but they also have a code and they have a hope and they do have this sense of humor. In Chandler, there's somewhat of a sense of humor, and a little bit in Hammett, too, but it's not as engaging as it is with Elmore. Those guys—the hardboiled guys—would write really hard, sharp, perceptive prose. Their dialogue has a pop to it. I think a relatively modern version of that, *Chinatown*—Robert Towne's dialogue in that sparkles and it engages you and it feels different and it feels real. But with Elmore's people, there was even more of a twinkle to it.

There's also sort of that way he would write in this present tense. "Jane walking into the room notes that blah, blah, blah...." I was an aspiring screenwriter back then, always trying my hand at writing a screenplay. Elmore's prose has a kind of pell-mell momentum built into it. You're just pulled along for the ride.

And then all of his rules.... He hadn't written down his rules yet, but you didn't have to skip much when you were reading Elmore. Even when it was getting to the climax and you really just wanted to find out what happens, he wrote it fast enough and terse enough that you could read every word and you'd still get the information you were dying to get in a prompt manner.

You ended up adapting the story Fire in the Hole. *What was it about that story in particular that inspired you to create Justified?*

GY: It was a bunch of things. First of all, there was a little bit of desperation that I needed something to do. I had a deal to write something for Sony, and the time was running out in the TV season when you could go out and pitch something. They sent me the story. Sarah Timberman and her partner, Carl Beverly, had optioned it. Or, Sony had optioned it for them, and they had gotten Michael Dinner to agree to direct it. So, there was already something in motion. They said, "Do you like Elmore Leonard?" And I said, "I *love* Elmore Leonard!" I'd never thought I would ever get a chance to adapt Elmore Leonard. They said, "We'll send you this story."

I read it and there were three things that got me. The big thing that it was Elmore Leonard. But then the fact that it wasn't set in Elmore's usual Miami or Detroit. I went, huh. Listen, Miami and Detroit are at least different enough. But more to the point, it wasn't set in L.A. or New York. But even more than that, it was not set in a major metropolitan area. Kentucky is a different part of the country. This is a different kind of world, and I don't know anything about this world, but he gets into it in this story and you get a feel for it and that's an interesting world.

Lastly, and the most important, I thought Raylan Givens could be the coolest character on television. It all came down to the scene in *Fire in the Hole* when he's at Ava's house and Dewey Crowe shows up and Raylan says, "You don't just walk into someone's house without being invited. You go out and we'll see." And Dewey says, "I'll go out and then I'm going to come right back in." And Raylan goes out and Dewey's got a shotgun pointed at him. Raylan says, "Can you rack a load before I put a hole in you?" He doesn't yell. There's no cop stuff; no "stop right there!" He's just got his hand on his gun and he just faces him down. I loved that guy. He's not freaking out, he's in control, but he's taking a gamble. But that's the way he does it. And then he says, "Because if I shoot you, I shoot to kill. There's no point in doing it otherwise." He just lays it out. And I thought, that's a character I'd love to write.

Just a little side note: when it came to writing that scene in the script for the pilot, I basically just wrote it exactly as Elmore did. I used as much of him as I could, word for word. Because why mess with the best?

And then lastly, if there's sort of an addendum to why I wanted to do it, it was because I had seen Elmore done right twice. I liked *52*

Pick-Up (1986). I know Elmore was not a big fan of it. But I think that was about a fifty to sixty-percent good Elmore movie. But the best were *Out of Sight* (1998) and *Get Shorty* (1995). Scott Frank, who adapted those, just let Elmore be Elmore. So that's what I did. Don't think you're going to write better dialogue than him. But if you are going to write dialogue that he didn't have, you'd better try to do it like him. Channel that, just as Elmore did when he was beginning as a writer and would try to channel [Ernest] Hemingway.

How did you end up with the title Justified?
GY: Absolutely no idea. It came from FX. We submitted a list of maybe twenty to thirty titles, none of which we were crazy about. We thought of calling the show *Raylan,* and we actually made a run at *Lawman.* We were headed towards that, and I don't know if a poster had been designed or any artwork, but then we started seeing billboards around town for a reality show starring Steven Seagal called *Lawman.* Well we can't use that. Even though we knew that show was going to disappear in a minute, they had it first. FX just came back, "What about *Justified*?" because there's a couple lines in the pilot where Raylan is asked, "Was that shooting justified?"

Fred Golan, who I had been working with for a long time, was one of the writers on *Justified.* He was the number two. He and I worked together on a show called *Boomtown* and another one called *Raines.* We're big fans of certain old Westerns. There's a great line in *Ride the High Country* (1962)—Sam Peckinpah's film—where there's talk about a man wanting to enter his father's house "justified." It's talking about when you die and you go to heaven, you want to enter God's house justified. So we said, "That's fine, because we're doing, in a way, a modern Western." Although Elmore said it wasn't.

Let's talk about the character Boyd Crowder. Boyd dies at the end of Elmore's original story, but you decided to keep him alive in the series. What factors led to that?
GY: We actually shot him dying. If you watch that scene, Raylan's looking down at him and Boyd says, "You shot me." And Raylan says, "Sorry." And Ava says, "Why did you say you were sorry?" And he says, "Well, we dug coal together." And Boyd dies! But when we tested it, the audience said, "Boy, that's a great character. It's too bad he's dead."

The other thing was we just loved the chemistry between the two of them (Tim and Walton) and felt that Boyd could be this dark mirror to Raylan. Boyd chose a different path, but that they were very similar growing up. Boyd went one way and Raylan went the other. And Boyd could always call Raylan on his bullshit. We felt that there were three people who could call Raylan on his bullshit—Boyd, Ava, and Winona (and Art, to a degree, because he knew him from before). Boyd perhaps most of all.

And lastly, and most importantly, it's Walton Goggins. He's just an amazing actor. Just to know that you're going to have that guy around.... Walton and I remember the moment well—I can remember where I was, and he can remember where he was—when I called him and said, "Hey, do you want to be part of the show?"

How difficult was it to justify—no pun intended—or find reasons to continue Raylan's and Boyd's relationship over six seasons without Raylan taking Boyd down?

GY: It was difficult. We would plan it season by season. So in the first season, Boyd is in custody and then he's out of custody. I said to the writer's room, "I'd love to end the season with Raylan and Boyd on the same side of a gun fight." So that's what we headed towards. So now they had a different kind of relationship.

In the second season, Boyd's not doing a lot of bad stuff. He's not back on Raylan's radar, although Raylan says, "You will be eventually because that's who you are." By the end of the season, Boyd is back.

But then in season three, Raylan's got bigger fish to fry. And the same with season four, and season five. We built season five to set up season six, so that the story would all came back to Raylan, Boyd, and Ava. That became our design once we decided the sixth season would be it. One of the big reasons we decided the sixth season would be it is because we knew that we were already right at the edge of repeating ourselves with Raylan and Boyd and that we would absolutely run out of real estate for the two of them. Seven seasons would've been too much. Five seasons might've been perfect, but six seasons worked.

Another magnificent decision you made was to keep Raylan's father alive and to actually put him in the story.

GY: There were a few other big decisions that we made in the pilot—decisions I made in the initial writing of the pilot and then that we made afterwards related to that. One was, I looked at Raylan and thought, if, in this modern world, he's wearing a cowboy hat and he's got his weapon on his hip and he's wearing cowboy boots, he's making a choice. How did he make that choice? Well, in the story, it talks about him watching movies; Gary Cooper, something like that. I decided, since we had to shift the timeline a little bit for Raylan's age and when Elmore wrote the story versus when we were set, it became him watching reruns of *Gunsmoke* on TV, with Marshal Dillon. Now Raylan's a marshal, so that works—he watched TV and made that choice. So I thought, why would somebody become so enamored of a fictional TV lawman? Well, he might if his father was a criminal. You go into law enforcement either because you come from a family of cops or because you're reacting against something. That's a truism, but it holds a certain amount of water. Okay, so his dad was a crook. What kind of crook? Then it just went from there.

There was a draft of the pilot where we had him have a scene with his father. Then I quickly decided no—if we're doing the series, we'll build to him. We'll create a legend. So that it's like *King Kong* (1933) where you don't see Kong for the first half hour of the movie. And that was that. That was the decision about the dad.

Another big decision was that he and Winona had not had children. We were making Raylan younger than Elmore had him. Elmore had him more forties, fifty. We're doing thirties and they hadn't had kids. That sort of changed the dynamic of Winona and her new husband. Went for something a little more upscale than the Winona and her new husband in the story. And also, have her in Lexington, so that they would see each other. That was a big choice.

And then the biggest thing, in many respects, was making it right for FX. FX, my joke with them was, "Oh, you guys won't be satisfied until the end of the pilot when Raylan goes into his basement and there's a 19-year-old boy chained to the wall." I mean, they love the dark turns and "oh my god, this person's a monster." So I said, "We're not going to do that." But I came up with the idea of him going to see Winona and scaring the shit out of Gary, and her saying, "Oh, honestly, Raylan, you're the angriest man I've ever known." And that look on his face of ... he knows it, but he doesn't know it, and he's surprised. The idea that this guy who's so cool and so in control has an underlying rage that could snap out—FX loved that. And Tim was able to play it for six years.

Raylan's character was much angrier on the show than he was in the novels. What made you decide to go that route?

GY: We needed somewhere to go for six seasons. The thing about writing a novel.... Elmore had a few characters come back, so he could dig into them some, but they really didn't change that much. Foley kind of does between *Out of Sight* (1996) and *Road Dogs* (2009), but they kind of stay the same. Elmore's view of characters is people are who they are. They aren't going to change that much. Tim and I agreed early on that Raylan would change over the course of the entire series maybe a millimeter, but it would be a critical millimeter. That was the long-term arc of Raylan. Him having to, without ever saying it, but having to look at and confront his anger was something we felt would sort of ground the character and give us someplace to go.

Elmore himself had some involvement with the show. What did his involvement entail?

GY: Elmore was a pro. He had been down this road before. He felt if he got paid, he didn't have to have any input. I've told this story many times, and it's true, is the only thing he objected to in the pilot was the hat. He didn't want a regular cowboy hat, he wanted what he called a Businessman's Stetson. But the hat we used looked good on Tim so that's how we went. But that's the reason why, at the very end of the series, Raylan's trademark hat gets a hole in it and he gets a new hat that's a little bit like the hat worn by the young gunfighter Boon. That's his new hat, and that hat is much closer to the hat that Elmore always wanted. So that was our little Elmore nod at the very end of the run.

The big thing Elmore did was write another book. Elmore came to visit in the first season and Tim was sitting with him on the set, and he said, "Elmore, have you thought of writing another Raylan story?" And Elmore said, "Ah! Maybe I will." So he wrote one, enjoyed himself, wrote another and then another, and then tied them together into his final book [*Raylan*]. The dedication page is probably one of the highlights for both Tim and me in our lives. We didn't know about it until we opened the book.

The novel is more of a sequel to the show than it is the other novels.

GY: [Laughs.] I mean, Boyd's alive!

Not many people can say they directly influenced the writing of Elmore Leonard. What is that like?

GY: If you don't mind profanity, it's fucking awesome! It's the coolest thing in the world. The fact that he liked the show was absolutely the highest compliment. He liked *Out of Sight* and he liked *Get Shorty* and he loved *Jackie Brown*. But when he would say that Tim was the best embodiment of any of his characters in film or television, that was pretty much the highest praise I think Tim could get.

I think it's an accurate statement, too.

GY: Yeah, I do too. Even though our Raylan is somewhat different from his Raylan, it felt like him. It was the spirit. You've probably heard the story of the rubber bracelets I got for the writers saying "WWED?" It was a joke, but that was our mantra: "What would Elmore do?" Honestly, we'd be in the room and we'd be banging against an idea, and we couldn't make something work, and we'd just stop and say, "Well, what would Elmore do?" After a certain point we didn't need to say it. We were all sort of thinking it. When we started the writers' room, we bought as many of Elmore's books as we could get our hands on and handed them out to all the writers.

One of the hardest things was episode two. Now what do we do? Now I'm not adapting. Now we've got to create something that feels like Elmore Leonard. "Well, we'll steal one scene." [Laughs.] We'll steal one scene from *Riding the Rap* where he's driving Dewey Crowe. We'll steal that. And Elmore says fine. But then we had to construct something with some wild characters, some who are stupid but some who have heart to them. We'll do something like that, and that became "Riverbrook."

Okay, at that point, that's me. I've written the pilot and the second episode. What happens when someone else writes it? One of the biggest growing pains in that first season was finding.... I knew Fred Golan could write it because he's just an incredibly talented, versatile writer. But I wasn't sure about anyone else, and it was a struggle. I had to do a lot of rewriting. One night, I had just finished rewriting one script, and I was looking at having to do a big rewrite on the next script, and I was up late and saying, "This is not sustainable." The next day I read an outline that Ben Cavell had sent in. He was one of the writers on staff. I read it and I got Fred in and I said, "Is this as good as I think it is?" And he said, "Yeah, it is." So immediately we put Ben on rewriting another script, and off we went. Now we had Ben, and we had Fred, and we had me. And then people got better at it. Wendy [Calhoun] got stronger. [Chris] Provenzano got better, so did Gary [Lennon]. Soon everyone on that staff just started to figure out what the show was. Even then, we made changes over the years and the writing staff changed.

The other big thing that happened that first year was, we couldn't get Dave Andron on staff. He was a writer Fred and I knew from *Raines*. He was on another show, but he was allowed to freelance two scripts for us. One of those was one of our best episodes that first year, "Hatless." That's the one where Raylan is suspended for a week, and Winona asks him to find out what's going on in her husband Gary's life. Dave was just fantastic with that script, and we ended up getting him on staff in the second season.

There was another writer, Taylor Elmore, that we knew from *Raines* who we thought might be right. He joined us in season 2 and he ended up being spectacular. Over the years, we assembled what we called the senior staff, which were the five guys who could really produce an episode and would help the younger writers along.

You've said in the past that you think at some points you guys might have actually gone beyond what Elmore would have in terms of dialogue.

GY: Well, I don't know if we ever went beyond, but we would try different things. If you watch the whole series and you're really paying attention to the dialogue, and you see who wrote it, you can tell a Ben Cavell episode from an Andron or Taylor Elmore or Provenzano or me or Fred or any number of the other writers. Especially Taylor Elmore. He really caught how poetic the dialogue could be. We all strove for that; he was really one of the best. There was some stuff that he would do, and maybe that's the closest to.... I would never say better than Elmore, but different in a really poetic way. And there was a point where we had to say, "Taylor, you have to rein that in. It's too much. We don't want to piss off Elmore." In our imagination Elmore was thinking, yeah guys, you've gone over the top. But we never seemed to have. He was always incredibly supportive.

He was extremely complimentary of the show. Beyond the hat, were there ever any instances where he gave you any sort of criticism?

GY: No. I honestly don't remember anything. I do remember the opposite of that, which is him sometimes saying, "I think you guys have done this better than I could've done it." There was a scene in the first season that he would always come back to. It was an episode that Wendy Calhoun wrote. It was a really fun episode—Ava gets kidnapped by the bad guys. There's a bit between Winona and Ava, the two women who've been romantically involved with Raylan. They run into each other and they sit on a bench in the courthouse. Winona knows who Ava is and Ava knows who Winona is. Elmore loved that scene. He loved the fact that they weren't sniping at each other. There was no sort of bitchiness. They were just two people who loved and had troubles with the same man. And they were just adults and they liked each other. They respected each other. He loved that scene. Wendy nailed that.

What was Elmore Leonard like, as a man, as you knew him?

GY: When he died I wrote a little tribute to him for the press kit. One of the lines was how one time when we went outside for a cigarette he said, "I think it's good you smoke." As I said, not many people were saying that to me in my life at that point. After the show, a year after doing *Sneaky Pete*, I did finally quit.

Elmore was wry. He was funny. He was genuine. He was just fun to be around. There was just that little sparkle. An elfish-ness. He had that sense of humor. And he loved to write. He loved to just sit in that office in his house, "The Embassy" as his kids called his house. Because it was this big house, and it had a pool and a tennis court. Anyway, he'd just sit in his office with a Virginia Slims in his hand. Oh, that was another thing I loved about him. He's a man and he smokes Virginia Slims and he doesn't give a shit that it's been marketed as a woman's cigarette. Like, fuck you, shut up! But he wouldn't even say that. He'd just go, "Well I don't care." The notion of him just running dialogue in his head, smoke trailing up from the cigarette.... Elmore loved to write. When it comes down to it, if you don't love to write, do something else.

Let's talk about doing the show after he died. Did his death have any effect on the way you approached things?

GY: People have said the fifth season was the weakest and have asked me if that was because it was the year that he died. No. I think there were other reasons that season didn't work as well. Interestingly enough, we were doing things in that season that were directly paying tribute to Elmore. We actually sent a crew to Florida to shoot for a few days for the opening episode where we meet the rest of the Crowe family. The fact that it focused on the Crowe family was a very Elmore thing because he loved that name and he loved that family. The fact that we had scenes in Detroit, we were paying tribute to the Detroit stories. Five had its ups and downs, and we were saddened by his death, but the man lived a great life.

When the family showed me the final page he was working on, I just lost it. They allowed me to take a picture of it and I've got it in my phone. I don't show it to anyone except on my phone. It was *Blue Dreams*, the novel he was working on about weed and Slab City and California. He was working on a scene where Raylan comes in to talk to Art

Mullen and Art says, "Maybe you should go to California and check into this thing." That was the last thing Elmore wrote. He was bringing Raylan into the story.

There were times when we thought about ending the whole series with Raylan being posted to California. The closest we came to that was having Raylan find Ava in California.

One last thing about Elmore's death—Tim and I, and Tim's wife, Alexis, went to the funeral outside of Detroit. Mike Lupica was there. He was one of Elmore's best friends, and he told this great story about calling up Elmore and asking, "So Elmore, what were you doing right now? Were you writing or were you thinking about girls?" And Elmore said, "Can't it be both?"

The first time I met Mike Lupica was in New York. Fred Golan and I were there with Elmore when *Justified* won a Peabody Award. We went out that night and we had dinner with Elmore, Mike Lupica, Greg Sutter, and William Goldman. As Hollywood writers who loved to hear stories about Hollywood writers, that was one of the highlights of the whole deal for Fred and me.

You mentioned the end of the show. I know that Raylan and Winona not ending up together made some fans mad, but I think that's very true to the spirit of Elmore's work.

GY: There's a wistfulness and a sadness often to the ends of his books. People don't get everything, but they get something. They're alive. There were a bunch of things we needed. The whole crutch was who was gonna live and who was gonna die. We didn't check it out with Greg Sutter. He knew Elmore and Elmore's work better than anyone. But when he saw the final episode he said Elmore would've loved it.

We just realized, first of all, the hero is not going to die. We're not going to kill Raylan. We're not going to kill Ava. The question was what's going to happen to Boyd? We thought, you know what, sometimes bad guys in his stories live. Especially if they're not horribly bad. The really sadistic guys? They die. But let's let Boyd live. And that just sort of led to "well, okay, what is the final season about?" It answers the question Raylan asks himself with Winona, at the end of the pilot, which is "if Tommy Bucks hadn't had a gun, would I still have shot him?"

So there he is in the barn with Boyd, and Boyd will not pick up the gun, and he basically says, "Shoot me." And Raylan doesn't shoot him. Raylan has every reason in the world to just fucking kill that guy because Boyd has done some awful, awful things. He transgressed the greatest thing you could do on *Justified*, which is he killed Dewey Crowe, for God's sake. Anyone who kills Dewey Crowe deserves to die! But Raylan doesn't kill him. That was the big thing.

Then I knew I wanted to do a time jump. I wanted to see where Raylan was. I wanted to pull a twist on the Winona thing. I wanted it to be sadder. I wanted it to be more bittersweet. You don't always get everything in life. But I wanted to see that she was okay and the daughter, little Willa, was okay. Jason Gedrick was nice enough to come in and play the new husband. We tried to get as many people from *Boomtown* on the show as we could over the years.

The other thing in Elmore's stories is that the women often get away with the money. I wanted Ava to be alive and well. And then there's the ending with Raylan and Boyd. It was Walton who said, "Hey, what if we came back to 'we dug coal together'?" I said, "That's the ticket. That's it."

I understand several of you went to Harlan before season two to research the area.

GY: That became a tradition. So every year after that, some writers would go. I only went that first time.

What were some of the things on the show that you think directly resulted from that?

GY: The big one was Mags Bennett. That was a game changer for us. That changed the whole series. That was a story about Mags Bailey, I believe her name was, and she was a criminal matriarch in Harlan and everybody loved her. She did some gnarly things, some bad shit, but people loved her. That, combined with the fact Elmore had written his *Raylan* book and we had read the advanced copy. In the book there was Purvis Crowe, and he was a weed farmer, and Raylan goes up against him and his boys. We immediately optioned the book, and Elmore said, "Just hang it up and strip it for parts." That understanding of how it works and what we need was one of his greatest gifts to the show. We plundered that book through season five. There were little bits that we would take, but we went at it big in season two and season three. The biggest thing was just taking Purvis Crowe and turning him into Mags Bennett.

Raylan, as portrayed by Timothy Olyphant, is a very iconic character. At this point it's difficult to imagine any other actor playing him. Was Timothy your first choice, or were there other people you looked at?

GY: One little side note: Raylan was played by another actor, and that was James LeGros in a Showtime version of *Pronto* (1997). He wore a hat that Elmore hated because it was such a big cowboy hat. James LeGros ended up playing a character for us, Wade Messer, who survived through seasons two, three, four, and died in five.

There were a couple of movie star type people we had thought of as Raylan. Woody Harrelson was a good idea. Woody Harrelson would've been a good Raylan. He wouldn't have been Tim. It would've been different. It would've been good. But he was going to be way too expensive, so we couldn't go that route.

Tim's name came up almost immediately because we knew he could wear a cowboy hat, we knew he could be scary, we knew he could be violent, we knew he could be funny, and we knew he could be romantic. He was the whole package. The middle one there was the most important one—he could be funny without being jokey. All of Elmore's characters have a sense of humor, the ones that work. If they don't, he either kills them off or they wander out of the story. So we always cast people who had a comic sensibility. And Tim was very much that.

He has a great smirk that really lends itself to that character.
GY: Yep. But the other thing was that he wasn't available. So that's why we were looking at other people. He was shooting a movie and wasn't going to be available until Memorial Day. And then finally, we just looked at ourselves, and said, "Let's wait." And we got Tim. It meant the show wouldn't come on until March, but that was okay. We were fine with that. We had our Raylan.

We talked a little bit about Scott Frank, who's written two terrific adaptations. Will we ever see another Graham Yost/Elmore Leonard project?
GY: Listen, we've talked about it and sometimes it'll come up. We'll meet occasionally and sort of toss things around. Without any false modesty or false pride, I think what we did we did very well. My fear is that trying to do it again, I wouldn't do it as well. For Scott, he wrote one movie and then he wrote another. Well, those are movies. They're two hours and then they're done. When you do seventy-eight hours of television, it's a big thing. So for me to even do an Elmore movie, it would be like, "Shit, it's gotta be as good as that series was." And to do another series is just too daunting. It's like, we've been. We've been and we did something we're really proud of. I don't want to, in any way, feel like I'm trading off of Elmore. And also, I don't want to tarnish what we've

done. We're proud of what we did. We think it's one of the best television shows of the era. But even that aside, we know that, at this point, it's the best version of Elmore Leonard's work that's been done for television. That's what John Landgraf wanted to do. That's what we all wanted to do.

This is a name that I only mentioned now, but it's a critical name. John Landgraf. He had been a producer and had co-written an episode of *Karen Sisco,* an earlier Elmore show, when he worked for Danny DeVito's company. When we pitched to FX, we knew that he was interested. My joke was, after I did my pitch and he then talked, I said, "John, if I knew what you were going to say, I would've pitched here first so I could've stolen what you just said for all the other pitches." He just got it. We knew that we could let Elmore be Elmore. That we could have long scenes. Scenes without the hero in it. Scenes just hanging out with criminals. We could just do that and do Elmore right. But he wanted to, as a legacy thing for him, to do the best Elmore Leonard show we could do. That's another part of the thing. We did that thing in that perfect time with the perfect head of a network and his team. It all just came together. The chance of it coming together again that well is unlikely.

Index

Index

Index

Index

184

Index

185

Index

Index

Scheider, Roy 18, 57
Schlitz Playhouse (television series) 97
Scott, Darin 95
Scott, Randolph 2, 103
Screenwriter 79
Seagal, Steven 169
Selby, Herbert, Jr. 161
Selleck, Tom 103
Sellers, Peter 138
Sellier, Chuck 102
"The Sense of Place in Elmore Leonard's Crime Fiction" (article) 70
Seven Men from Now (film) 103
Seven Slayers (novel) 112
77 Sunset Strip (television series) 141
"The Shadow of Your Smile" (song) 94
Shaeffer, Jack 98
Shameless (television series) 79, 128
Shamus Award 9, 46
Shane (novel) 98
Shepard, Joan 88
"Shot in the Dark" International Crime Writers Award 107
Shotgun (novel) 95
Showtime (network) 79, 178
Siegel, Michael 149
Sigman, Stephanie 76, 78
Silent Night, Deadly Night (film) 102
Silicon Valley (television series) 76
Singleton, John 21
Six Guns and Slay Bells (anthology) 95
The Six Million Dollar Man (television series) 102
"Slant-Six" (story) 55
Slater, Christian 125, 130
Slide (novel) 15
Sneaky Pete (television series) 166, 175
Songs of Innocence (novel) 7
Sonnenfeld, Barry 80, 81
Sons of Sam Spade (nonfiction book) 65
Sony 23, 28
The Sopranos (television series) 82, 83
Speed (film) 166
Spenser for Hire (television series) 19
Spielberg, Steven 166
Split Images (novel) 7, 70
Starbucks 136
Stark, Richard (pseudonym) 58
Starr, Jason 15, 53
Steel, Danielle 4
Steely Dan 90
Steinbeck, John 44, 165
Stella, Charlie 3, 15, 160–165
Stick (film) 8, 69, 90
Stick (novel) 7, 10, 11, 13, 69, 99
Stollman, Lee 151
Stout, Rex 53

Sturges, John 103
Sun Classics Pictures 102
The Sunshine Boys (film) 131
Supporting Characters (film) 147
Sutter, Greg 36, 37, 74, 106, 143, 176
Swag (novel) 7, 56, 132, 135, 145, 164, 167
Swanson, H.N. 2
SWAT (television series) 76
Sweeney, Julia 21
Sweet Dreams (novel) 123
The Switch (novel) 7, 121, 147, 148, 150, 153, 156, 157, 159

The Taking of Pelham One Two Three (film) 130, 131
The Tall T (film) 2, 54, 97, 101, 103
Tarantino, Quentin 2, 3, 11, 13, 17, 21, 33, 39, 45, 58, 59, 60, 69, 113, 121, 147, 150, 151, 152, 154, 156
"10 Rules of Writing" (article) 3, 45, 111
10 Rules of Writing (nonfiction book) 8
The Texas Literary Hall of Fame 107
These Violent Times (novel) 95
Thomas, Isiah 35, 38
Thompson, Jim 15, 47
3lbs (television series) 79
3:10 to Yuma (film, 1957) 2, 21, 22, 23, 24, 27, 30, 54, 75, 103
3:10 to Yuma (film, 2007) 21–34, 75, 105
"3:10 to Yuma" (story) see "Three-Ten to Yuma"
"Three-Ten to Yuma" (story) 2, 21, 96, 100
Three-Ten to Yuma and Other Stories (collection) 7
Thuglit: Last Writes (anthology) 55
Timberman, Sarah 168
Time 1
A Time for Violence (anthology) 105
Tishomingo Blues (novel) 7
TNT (network) 103
Tolstoy, Leo 142
Tombstone (film) 22
"The Tonto Woman" (story) 45, 100
The Tonto Woman and Other Western Stories (collection) 7
The Toronto International Film Festival 147, 152
Toronto Raptors 38
The Toronto Star 35, 40
Toth, Frannie 143
Touch (novel) 7, 70, 138, 139
Towne, Robert 167
Trail of the Apache and Other Stories (collection) 7
Trancers (film series) 95
Trancers III (film) 95
Travolta, John 83, 127, 128, 130, 131
Trinity College 166

187

Index